Virtually all men I know  lessness in their strugg
pandemic in our world
a clear, gospel anchored way to fight the fight and lay aside
the weight and the sin that so easily ensnares us.

Bob Lepine, cohost, FamilyLife Today

Indulging in pornography is an international pandemic
that will send you to hell. Is it worth it to pursue a fleeting
pleasure that is God-defying, life-wasting, family-betraying,
poison-injecting, mind-ruining, conscience-searing, and
slavery-fueling? The wise advice in this book is a gift for
two groups of people: those who are struggling and those
who want to help.

Andy Naselli, associate professor of systematic theology
and New Testament for Bethlehem College and Seminary
in Minneapolis and a pastor of Bethlehem Baptist Church

The problem is deeper than the problem. That's the message of *More than a Battle*. Joe Rigney explains how our
struggle with lust and pornography is in fact an expression
of our original good desire for love, success, fulfillment,
and happiness, a desire now twisted and distorted by the
Fall. To address the whole problem, Rigney argues that we
must both starve the sinful cravings by denying the temptations of the flesh, and feed the original good desire, by pursuing our earthly vocation and our spiritual duty. And all
must be done in the desire and expectation that God will
satisfy our greatest desires. *More than a Battle* combines

this theory with practice, as it offers concrete suggestions for developing practices and habits that form lasting virtue. This is a book for all Christians currently fighting the world, the flesh, and the devil.

Steven Wedgeworth, associate pastor of Faith Presbyterian Church (PCA) in Vancouver, British Columbia

To be confronted by one's sin is a severe mercy. There can be no repentance and no glory to come if we are not confronted by our sin, and yet the confrontation can be immensely painful. I hope that every Christian trapped in the mires of sexual sin has a mentor to guide them with the hopefulness, shrewdness, and graciousness Rigney displays in this book. *More than a Battle* is not just a helpful guide for Christians mired in sexual sin, though it certainly is that. It's also a perceptive study of the human heart that equips readers to understand their sin more carefully and to combat it more intelligently. It helps readers see that chastity is beautiful. And it's a remarkable application of the gospel to the lives of sinful people. This will be a go-to guide for pastors, campus ministers, and lay people alike.

Jake Meador, author of *In Search of the Common Good* and editor-in-chief of *Mere Orthodoxy*

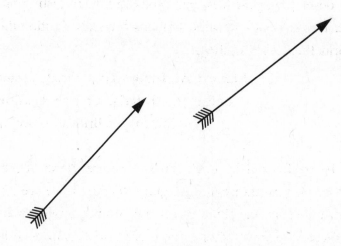

MORE
THAN A
BATTLE

How to Experience Victory,
Freedom, and Healing from Lust

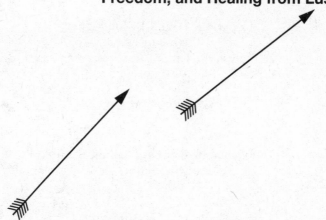

MORE
THAN A
BATTLE

Joe Rigney

B&H
PUBLISHING
NASHVILLE, TENNESSEE

Published by B&H Publishing Group
Nashville, Tennessee

Dewey Decimal Classification: 176
Subject Heading: PORNOGRAPHY / EROTICA /
SEXUAL ETHICS

Cover design and illustration by B&H Publishing Group.

2 3 4 5 6 7 8 • 26 25 24 23 22

To the men of Cities Church

Contents

Acknowledgments   xi

Introduction   1

1   Walk by the Spirit   15

2   Starve the Beast   33

3   How Do Humans Work?   49

4   Presenting the Body and Renewing
the Mind   67

5   The Longer War   87

6   The Wider War   101

7   The Deeper War   113

8   Sexual Brokenness   125

9   The Subtler War   135

10   A Word to Young Men–
Single, Dating, and Engaged   153

11   A Word to Married Men–
The Watchdog and the Caged Animal   169

12   A Word to Married Men–
Nuisance Lust and Marital Intimacy   187

13   A Final Exhortation   201

Appendix: Further Resources   207

Acknowledgments

This book was born from relationships. It was born from conversations, counseling sessions, conference messages, pastoral interventions, small groups, friendships, and mentoring relationships. When I was in college, Bill Biggs played a pivotal role in modeling compassionate stability to me (before I even knew what that was). I heard David Powlison deliver a life-transforming conference message on "Making All Things New" at the 2004 Desiring God Conference for Pastors. In 2013, Bethlehem Baptist Church hosted the Pure Pleasure Conference for men. The conference was the brainchild of my friend Kempton Turner, who felt burdened over the devastation of pornography among the men at Bethlehem. Kempton delivered two powerful messages on fighting the pleasure of lust with superior pleasure in Christ. I was given the privilege of doing four follow-up sessions with men in which we sought to apply gospel strategies in the fight against lust. Those four sessions eventually became the heart of this book.

In 2016, I gave the same four sessions to the men at Cities Church. We incorporated the sessions into our discipleship structures in hopes of fostering a community of men who are able to help one another fight the fight of faith. The feedback from those sessions led me to believe that there might be room for a book designed to help whole churches approach the struggle against pornography and sexual sin in a biblically grounded, holistic, and practical way.

As the book came together, a number of friends offered insights and feedback on how to improve it. Some of them gave extensive feedback and offered help on the structure of the book itself. I'm deeply grateful to Samuel James, Andy Naselli, Justin Dillehay, Clayton Hutchins, Zach Krych, Mike Schumann, Aaron Bryant, Devin Mork, Cody Sandidge, Josh Bremerman, Paul Poteat, Jeff Evans, and Greg Morse for taking the time to read through the project (in various forms) and help me make it better. I'm especially grateful for the feedback of Warren Watson. Warren's approach to counseling has profoundly shaped my own, and his interaction with the book has brought out additional dimensions of soul care that I never would have recognized on my own.

As always, I'm deeply grateful for my fellow pastors at Cities Church: Nick Aufenkamp, David Easterwood, Josh Foster, Kevin Kleiman, David Mathis, Jonathan Parnell, Mike Polley, and Michael Thiel. Serving alongside these men in ministry is one of the great privileges of my life. They have influenced all aspects of my ministry, and their fingerprints show up in a variety of ways throughout this book.

Finally, I don't have words to express my gratitude to my wife, Jenny. She was a powerful means of grace that the Lord used in helping me experience victory, freedom, and healing from sin. Her influence is everywhere in this book. Through her patience, grace, and wisdom, she has helped me know myself more deeply. More importantly, she has helped me know God more deeply. And that has made all the difference.

Introduction

If you're picking up this book, it's likely because you or someone you know has a problem. That problem goes by various names: Sexual sin. Pornography. Masturbation. Lust.

I don't know what led you to this book. Maybe you're fed up with yourself and looking for anything to help you overcome an addiction to pornography. Maybe someone recommended this book to you. Maybe they even gave you a copy. Maybe you're in an accountability group that is going to work through it. Maybe you're leading a group like that and want to be better equipped to help men who struggle. Maybe you're a pastor who wants to help the men in your church grow in holiness and obtain victory over this "sin that so easily ensnares" (Heb. 12:1).

Whatever the reason, if you sincerely want to be delivered from the chains of pornography and sexual sin, or if you want to help those who are bound by those chains, then I believe this book can help. I've used the strategies outlined here in my ministry for fifteen years. More than that, this book is the fruit of my own decade-long struggle with lust in my teenage years and God's grace in delivering me from it. Let me tell you a little bit about that.

My Story

My struggle with sexual sin began when I was about thirteen years old. This was the pre-smartphone, pre-Wi-Fi 1990s, back in the days when a boy's first exposure to porn often happened when a friend brought his dad's *Playboy* to school to show everyone. That's what happened to me.

When I was in seventh grade, a friend brought the magazine, and a group of us stood around in a circle in the alley behind the school, wide-eyed and fascinated by the glossy pictures of naked women. Compared to the way most kids today encounter pornography, it could be considered tame. But it still had a profound effect on my hormonally charged mind and body.

In eighth grade, I saw my first pornographic video at a sleepover. After the parents were in bed, one of the guys turned on HBO's late-night programming, and we sat there in the dark, again wide-eyed, fascinated, and aroused by what was happening on screen. From there my interest grew and expanded. I acquired my own stash of magazines. And though we didn't have HBO, there was still plenty of sexually charged material on late-night TV to enflame the desires of a teenage boy.

And then the Internet happened.

All of a sudden, I had access to all kinds of images on the World Wide Web. And when I was home by myself, I took advantage of that access and learned how to cover my tracks. Later, on a school trip in high school, a group of us were staying in a hotel room, and I got my first exposure to hard-core pornography, the kind you have to pay for. The images impressed themselves on my mind, and the memories lingered in my imagination for years.

My enslavement grew through high school and into college, as I learned to navigate the various corners of the Internet, seeking more and more videos and images to gratify my desires. And through it all, the arousal and addiction were wedded to a deep sense of shame and guilt at what I was doing. As a Christian, I knew God called me to purity and holiness, but my life was marked by the opposite. Lust and pornography had me by the throat, and I felt powerless in the face of the raging desires that would awaken in my heart, mind, and body.

> As a Christian, I knew God called me to purity and holiness, but my life was marked by the opposite.

Don't get me wrong. I tried all sorts of methods to break free. Accountability groups in high school, conferences and special events devoted to pursuing purity, books on how to fight sexual sin—I tried them all, repeatedly, with varying measures of temporary success. But it wasn't until I was engaged to my wife that something finally broke. Over the course of a year, I experienced a fundamental shift in my life and my fight with sexual sin. God broke through in a powerful way, and the struggle was never the same. Not that I'm completely free from sexual temptation and sin—that will have to wait for glory. But since that time, I've been delivered from pornography and masturbation (even as there were lingering emotional effects on my first year of marriage from the decade of bondage).

Looking back, I can see a number of factors the Lord used to accomplish that fundamental transformation. For starters, marriage raised the stakes. No longer could I pretend that lust was only about me. There was another human being involved, one I deeply loved and cared for and who would be devastated by my continued failure. By raising the stakes, marriage provided a crucial motivation for pursuing holiness.

In a similar way, my acceptance into seminary and my call to ministry played a key role in motivating me to fight in a way I never had. I knew that pornography use would not only wreck my marriage, it would disqualify me from ministry. So, in that window of time, the Lord provided two real and concrete motivations to pursue purity with a fresh zeal.

But increased motivation wasn't enough. I also needed greater measures of wisdom in knowing myself, how I worked, and what was underneath my struggle. The Lord provided that as well. The pastor who did our premarital counseling proved invaluable in unearthing layers and depths in my own heart and mind. His wisdom and counsel helped steer the newfound motivation in a fruitful direction. He helped me gather up much of the wisdom from all of those books and conference messages over the years and put them to better use. With his help and the grace of God, I had a fresh resolve and determination to grow in wisdom and knowledge of God and myself–to learn how the gospel met me with my particular history, temptations, and patterns. And though it wasn't easy, the change was real and unmistakable.

Since that time, I've continued to grow in my understanding of the struggle with lust and pornography as I've taught and mentored students and pastored and counseled the men of my church. Over the last fifteen years, I've added more tools to my tool belt, filling out the biblical, theological, and psychological foundation beneath the strategies and practices I use in my own life and commend to others. This book is an attempt to describe the gospel-grounded principles and practices that enabled me to gain victory over lust, to break free from addiction to pornography, and to heal the wounds of my sexual failures. Because the fight against lust and pornography has never been more difficult.

Three Lenses

We live in an age of unprecedented access to sexual sin. Of course, sexual temptation itself is as old as dirt. Debauchery, immorality, and temptation have been around since the fall of man. But they haven't always been so easy to access.

First-century Christians had to deal with temple prostitution. Victorians faced brothels. But not every person had a brothel in their pocket. Nor did they have to face life-size, crystal clear, photoshopped images of women in lingerie any time they wanted to pick up some milk at Target. Our society's obsession with sex, coupled with the technologies that make pornography so accessible, means it's never been more difficult to flee sexual immorality and pursue holiness. The result is that our families, our churches, and our society are being devastated by a pornography epidemic.

>>>————————▶

It's never been more difficult to flee sexual immorality and pursue holiness.

◀————————《《《

But what should we do about this epidemic? How should we address the challenge of pornography and lust in our own day? In my experience, approaches to this struggle can basically be broken down into three categories. Think of these as three lenses for viewing the fight.

1. **Sexual sin as immorality.** This approach accents our culpability and wickedness in pursuing sinful pleasures, as we are willingly led astray by our sinful desires. Our aim in the struggle is to renounce evil desires, repent of

shameful actions, and put to death the deeds of the body. The fundamental call is to fight a war against sinful passions.

2. **Sexual sin as addiction.** This approach accents the bodily and enslaving dimension of the struggle, as chemicals and hormones hijack and rewire our brains. Our aim is to unmask the lies of sexual addiction, to seek freedom from destructive patterns, and to break the habits that enslave us. The fundamental call is to struggle for liberation from sin's mastery.

3. **Sexual sin as brokenness.** This approach accents the deep wounds sexual dysfunction reveals. We pursue short-term sexual pleasure as a way of coping with unmet needs, family dysfunction, trauma, and abuse. Our aim in the struggle is to pursue renewal and transformation by renarrating our stories and repairing the ruins of past pains and sorrows. The fundamental call is to heal the wounds of our sexual brokenness.

Most books on this subject at least acknowledge the value of each of these lenses. However, usually one lens is taken to be more fundamental and, as a result, the other two are neglected.

Frequently, counselors and pastors will issue warnings about the lenses they view as less important. For example, those who view sexual sin through the lens of brokenness are sometimes wary of emphasizing the evil and shame of sexual immorality, since the increased guilt prevents the individual from pursuing healing for the true causes beneath his or her broken desires. On the other hand, those who see sexual sin fundamentally as immorality worry that emphasizing the addictive element blames the sin on the body and the brain and lessens the responsibility for repentance and sin-killing.

For my own part, I think we ought to see significant value in all three lenses. All three can be of enormous help for the struggling sinner. My own tendency is to default to the language of war, violence, and struggle. This is partly because the Bible regularly uses this sort of language (Matt. 5:27–30; Rom. 8:13; Col. 3:5) and partly because it's how I've grown accustomed to resisting the pull of sexual temptation in my own life. But, as the title of this book indicates, I am convinced that this is more than a battle, more than a war. Thus, I don't want to ignore the bodily and addictive element or the role of brokenness, trauma, and pain in fueling sexually immoral desires and behavior. I've seen firsthand that the language of war, battle, and violence has a tendency to create the wrong kind of pressure in the fight, often leading to more shame and guilt. I've also seen that wise warfare often involves de-escalating situations and pursuing indirect assaults. (More on all of this later in the book.) But my fundamental point is that each lens brings something valuable to the table and that the more holistic our approach to this struggle, the better we'll be able to fight sin in our own lives and to help others break free from bondage to unwanted sexual desire.

> The more holistic our approach to this struggle, the better we'll be able to fight sin in our own lives and to help others break free from bondage to unwanted sexual desire.

I mention these three lenses here because the banner I wave over my entire approach to this struggle is Galatians 5:16: "I say, then, walk by the Spirit and you will certainly not carry out the desire of the flesh." That's what we're after: walking by the Spirit. And the Spirit of God addresses us in our immorality, in our bondage, and in our brokenness.

- We are called to put to death the deeds of the body by the Spirit (Rom. 8:13) and so we *wage war* by the Spirit.
- "Where the Spirit of the Lord is, there is freedom" (2 Cor. 3:17) because the Spirit is the one who sets us free from the law

of sin and death (Rom. 8:2); and so we
are *set free* by the Spirit.

- In the book of Isaiah, the Spirit is the one
  who anoints the Messiah to bind up the
  brokenhearted, to comfort the mourn-
  ing, and to give them a garment of praise
  instead of a faint spirit (Isa. 61:1–4), so
  we are *healed* by the Spirit.

Therefore, in the struggle with sexual immorality,
addiction, and brokenness, we must learn to walk by the
Spirit, who kills our sin, sets us free, and heals our wounds.

How to Use This Book

This book is designed for two different groups: men
who are presently struggling with lust and pornography
and men who want to help them. Many books on the fight
with sexual sin are targeted at the first group. My approach
is a little bit different. It's birthed out of our church's phi-
losophy of ministry: to equip the saints for the work of
ministry. Given the challenge posed by pornography in
our culture, it's crucial that men support and challenge one
another in the fight rather than relying exclusively on pastors to address the issues. So at our church we've sought to
provide teaching and resources to our men that will foster
a growing culture of wisdom and godliness, enabling them
to help and exhort one another in this struggle.

Thus, I've written this book as though I were addressing a group of men who are seeking to grow in wisdom
and godliness together. This group is made up of those
who are presently struggling and those who are seeking
to help them. Sometimes I'll address the mentors directly–
it'll be clear when I'm doing this, marked off as "A Note to
Mentors." Other times, I'll address those who are in the
thick of the fight. Often, I'll simply address the group as a
whole.

The best way to use this book is to read the chapters
individually and then come together with a group to discuss what resonated with you. After that, you can develop
strategies and applications for your own situation.

Additionally, I've written this book primarily for men.
As a man, I have a better understanding of the temptations and struggles of men than I do of the struggles of
women. As a result, most of my ministry in this area has
been to men. Nevertheless, I pray that women who struggle with pornography and lust will find this book helpful
as well.

This book will be helpful for women who want to
understand the struggles facing their husbands or their
sons. In fact, there are certain sections I would encourage husbands and wives to read together and discuss. And
given how widespread pornography is, and the simple fact
that children are encountering it at such a young age, it's
vital that fathers and mothers have a shared understanding
of the fight their sons (and daughters) are facing and that

they are able to offer them wisdom and strategies in resisting temptation and dealing with failure.

However you use this book, I'm just glad you're using it. I hope it will be a helpful tool in your tool belt. My prayer is that the Spirit of God would use this book to grant you victory, freedom, and healing or that the Spirit would use this book to bring victory, freedom, and healing through you to someone you love.

A Note to Pastors and Church Leaders

I've tried to design this book with congregations in mind. My hope is that it can be part of a long-term strategy for men's discipleship in your church. Think of the good that would come if, over time, dozens of men in your church are capable of providing counsel and wisdom to other men. Think of the impact on the families in your community. Think of the devastation you might spare the next generation. Therefore, I want to encourage you to take Jethro's advice to Moses in Exodus 18:18: *if you try to do it alone, you'll wear yourself out.* Instead, identify capable and godly men in your midst and train them to handle the basics, leaving you to handle the heavier cases. Throughout the book, I've included sections called "A Word to Mentors" that go into greater detail on some of the theological foundations underneath the strategies. At the end, I've included an appendix with resources for further study. As you have more men available to mentor others, you can direct them to these resources for further equipping. Personal holiness is a community project, and men must lead the way.

1

Walk by the Spirit

Much of this book will be devoted to practical strategies for fighting sexual sin. However, it's important that our practical strategies are grounded in the Word of God. In the introduction I mentioned Galatians 5:16 and described it as a banner that flies over this whole book. So here at the outset, let's take some time and dig into the passage and try to understand just what Paul promises.

> I say, then, walk by the Spirit and you will certainly not carry out the desire of the flesh. For the flesh desires what is against the Spirit, and the Spirit desires what is against the flesh; these are opposed to each other, so that you don't do what you want. But if you are led by the Spirit, you are not under the law.
>
> Now the works of the flesh are obvious: sexual immorality, moral impurity, promiscuity, idolatry, sorcery, hatreds, strife,

jealousy, outbursts of anger, selfish ambitions, dissensions, factions, envy, drunk-
enness, carousing, and anything similar. I
am warning you about these things—as I
warned you before—that those who practice
such things will not inherit the kingdom of
God.

But the fruit of the Spirit is love, joy,
peace, patience, kindness, goodness, faithfulness, gentleness, and self-control. The
law is not against such things. Now those
who belong to Christ Jesus have crucified
the flesh with its passions and desires. If
we live by the Spirit, let us also keep in step
with the Spirit. (vv. 16–25)

For many years, I misunderstood this passage, especially the relationship between verse 16 and verse 17. Verse
16 contains an exhortation ("walk by the Spirit") and a
promise ("and you will certainly not carry out the desire
of the flesh"). In fact, it contains a *staggering* promise. The
"not" in the promise is intensified in the original Greek; it's
what's called an emphatic negation. Paul essentially says,
"If you walk by the Spirit, you will *absolutely and certainly
not* gratify the desires of the flesh." And of course, gratifying the *desires* of the flesh is unpacked in the *works* of the
flesh in verses 19–21. That list begins with sexual immorality, sensuality, and impurity and ends with orgies and

things like these. The passage, then, is clearly relevant for the struggle with sexual sin. And, like I said earlier, Paul leads with an incredible promise.

But then, after making this staggering promise, Paul seems to walk it back. He says that fleshly desires and spiritual desires are at war and that the hostility between them keeps us from doing the things we want. For the longest time I read that as an amazing promise, followed by a dose of realism, as though Paul were saying, "Walk by the Spirit and you absolutely will not gratify fleshly desires! (Except that, actually, you kinda will gratify the desires of the flesh; you're frequently going to be frustrated in your attempts at holiness.)" The war between the flesh and the Spirit, I thought, would prevent any lasting victory. So I expected to permanently live in the midst of frustrated and hostile desires.

Put another way, I used to read Galatians 5:16–17 as basically a summary of Romans 7, where Paul describes the internal conflict between the part of him that loves and agrees with God's law and the part of him that rejects and rebels against it. In that passage Paul is confused by his actions; he agrees with God's law, but then he does the thing he hates. His good desires are frustrated by his inability to carry them out.[1] That's what I thought Galatians 5 was teaching as well: good intentions frustrated by sin and failure.

---

[1] See "A Word to Mentors: What About Romans 7?" on page 29 for my understanding of that passage.

I never thought too deeply about why Paul bothered with the staggering promise of deliverance in verse 16 if our actual experience is ongoing frustration of our godly desires. But since I felt frustrated in my fight with sin, I just accepted the frustration and failure as part of the normal Christian life.

Rightly Understanding Paul's Logic

In seminary, a classmate challenged my understanding of Paul's logic. He demonstrated that one way to better understand the flow of Paul's thought is to read verses 16 and 17 in reverse order while keeping the logical relationship intact. He turned an "A, because B" argument into a "B, therefore A" argument. When we do that, the passage looks like this:

> (Verse 17) For the flesh desires what is against the Spirit, and the Spirit desires what is against the flesh; these are opposed to each other, so that you don't do what you want.

> (Verse 16) [THEREFORE] (that's the logical connection) walk by the Spirit, and you will certainly not carry out the desire of the flesh.

Note the difference. In my original reading, our destination is ongoing warfare and frustration; it's the realistic walk-back after the amazing promise. We start with high hopes and ambitions but eventually come back to the reality of frustrated attempts at holiness. On the second reading, the warfare and frustration are the starting point, and the amazing promise is the destination. The exhortation ("walk by the Spirit") is the bridge between them.

In other words, Paul is actually saying something like this: "As a Christian, you wake up every day in the midst of a war. Fleshly desires pull you in one direction; the desires of the Spirit pull you in the other. The status quo is a frustrated stalemate. Spiritual desires frustrate fleshly desires, and fleshly desires frustrate spiritual desires." But into that frustration and war, Paul issues a call and makes a promise: "If, in the midst of this war, you walk by the Spirit, if you seek to live by the Spirit's power and gratify his desires, then you will absolutely and certainly not gratify those fleshly desires that are so frustrating to you right now."

Reversing the order to clarify the logic made all the difference in understanding the passage. Not only does the second reading make better sense of the passage, but I also found it to be pastorally fruitful, especially for addressing issues like sexual sin and pornography.

In these short verses, Paul gives us a threefold vision of the daily Christian life. First, Galatians 5:16–17 means that we can clearly recognize and own the reality and difficulty of the war. That's where we all start. It's probably why you picked up this book. You feel the frustration of the war. And Paul's words encourage us to be honest about where we are. Think about your own experience of sexual sin. Have you felt the competing desires Paul describes? The frustration? The sense of being stuck? How long has it been going on? Have there been significant victories? Major defeats? Where are the pressing battles today?

So the frustration of the war is where we all start. But according to Paul, we don't have to stay there because, second, we have a new destination. We can live a life where we absolutely don't gratify the desires of the flesh. Now it's important to be clear about what Paul is and isn't promising. He's not saying our fleshly desires disappear altogether. Instead, he promises that we will not *carry out or gratify* or *complete* those desires. In other words, the desires may still be present and still at war with spiritual desires, but now, as we walk by the Spirit, we won't indulge them. The basic idea is that all desires have a direction, a destination, a trajectory. When that destination is reached, the desire has been gratified. The itch has been scratched. But the presence of the desire doesn't mean we have to indulge it. It's possible to resist where our desires want to take us. For Paul, walking by the Spirit doesn't remove all fleshly tendencies and trajectories in this life. Instead, it interrupts them. It redirects them and reorders them so that they no longer dishonor God or harm people. And it's important to be clear on this point so that we don't create impossible and unrealistic expectations for the Christian life. In this life the desires may still arise, but according to Paul, they don't have to master us. We don't have to gratify or indulge them. We can be free.

But only if we walk by the Spirit. That's the third element in Paul's vision of the Christian life in Galatians 5. Walking by the Spirit is the bridge between our present struggle and the future victory. It's the path that gets us

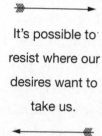

It's possible to resist where our desires want to take us.

from frustration to freedom. Which means that the pressing question for us is this: *What exactly does it mean to "walk by the Spirit"?*

Position, then Progress

In one sense this whole book is an attempt to answer that question. "Walking by the Spirit" is the banner that flies over the whole project. For now, let me make one important distinction that is crucial for thinking about the Christian life.

Throughout Paul's letters, he distinguishes between our fundamental *position* before God and our ongoing *progress* in holiness. God declares us to be righteous in Christ (position) and then we seek to walk righteously in the world (progress). God adopts us as sons into his family (position) and then calls us to walk as obedient sons

rogress). God decisively sets us apart for his
purposes (position) and then calls us to daily walk in those
purposes (progress). God definitively delivers us from the
dominion of sin (position) and then calls us to live as free
men (progress).

Galatians 5:25 is a clear example of this paradigm: "If
we live by the Spirit, let us also keep in step with the Spirit."
That is, if we possess life by the Spirit (position), then let us
walk in rhythm with the Spirit (progress).

There's a similar pattern underneath Paul's question in
Galatians 3:3: "After beginning by the Spirit, are you now
finishing by the flesh?" Paul assumes there's a decisive
beginning to the Christian life (often called "conversion").
It happens when the Spirit opens our eyes to believe that
Jesus lived, died, and rose again for us and our salvation.
This beginning settles our position before God. We're righteous. We're accepted. We're God's sons. We're free. Paul
points to this decisive moment when he says, "I have been
crucified with Christ, and I no longer live, but Christ lives
in me" (Gal. 2:20).

And then the rest of the Christian life is an attempt
to live in and live out of that fundamental truth. In other
words, we seek to be perfected and completed, to grow into
the fullness of salvation over the course of our lives. And
Paul's point in Galatians 3:3 is that, just as we began by the
Spirit, so also, we will be perfected by the Spirit.

With the distinction between position and progress in
mind, "walking by the Spirit" refers to the progress side of

the equation. It refers to a lifestyle, a conduct, a way of living and acting in the world that is guided by, governed by, and sustained by the Spirit of the living God.

Paul has a number of ways to describe this ongoing lifestyle and conduct. In Galatians 2:14, Paul says there is a conduct that is "deviating from the truth of the gospel." The gospel says that Jews and Gentiles are made right with God in the same way—by faith in Jesus. So when Peter withdraws from table fellowship with Gentile Christians, his conduct doesn't fit the gospel. He's not "walking rightly" in the truth of the gospel. His walk doesn't match his talk. His conduct doesn't match his profession.

Later in Galatians, Paul says that we are "led by the Spirit" (Gal. 5:18). God's Spirit guides us the way he guided the Hebrews through the wilderness with a pillar of fire and cloud in the book of Exodus. And, as I noted earlier, Paul also urges us to "keep in step with the Spirit" (Gal. 5:25). Elsewhere he urges us to "walk worthy of the calling you have received" (Eph. 4:1) and prays that we would "walk worthy of the Lord" (Col. 1:10). Other similar phrases in the Bible include walking in love, walking in the light, walking as children of the light, walking according to Paul's example, and walking in the truth.

In all of these examples, the idea is the same: there is a conduct, a "walking" that accords with the gospel, with the Spirit, with the truth. There is a way of life that fits the gospel. There is a natural resonance between this way of life and the truth of the gospel of Jesus Christ. That's not to say that godly conduct *is* the gospel, but that wherever the gospel is authentically present, this lifestyle will be evident and growing. Wherever the gospel is planted in a human heart, walking by the Spirit is the inevitable fruit.

>>>————————▶

Wherever the gospel is planted in a human heart, walking by the Spirit is the inevitable fruit.

◀————————«

So then, keep the distinction between position and progress in mind as we pursue the practical strategies in this book. Position, then progress. Life, then lifestyle. Conversion, then conduct. Possessing life by the Spirit, then walking by the Spirit. Gospel roots, then gospel fruit.

The Challenge of Applying the Gospel

This distinction is crucial for making progress in all forms of holiness, and especially sexual purity. But in making this distinction, we need to be aware of two dangers as we seek to apply the gospel to our lives.

The first danger is that we can try to detach the conduct from the gospel. We can try to walk as sons of God apart from the felt reality that we *are* sons of God through faith in Jesus. This is the danger of *legalism*, the danger of bare commands. It's the danger of empty moralism that seeks

to create godly conduct with no reference to gospel realities. And of course, this doesn't work because rootless trees
don't bear good fruit. We must have gospel life coursing
through our veins if we want to have gospel conduct coming out our fingertips.

This isn't to say that legalism never overcomes sexual immorality. Sometimes it does. I've known men who
have attained a significant measure of victory over sexual
sin through their own efforts. But what is the result? The
men who may have emptied themselves of pornography
and masturbation are simply filled, on the other side, with
pride and arrogance. They don't boast in the Lord; they
boast in their "success." But the reality is, they have simply
exchanged one sin for another, and the devil is more than
happy to make that trade.

The other danger is more subtle, and it is especially relevant for people who are aware of the legalistic danger. It is
the danger, not of pure command without the gospel, but
of *bare repetition* of the gospel. Legalism tries to clean the
corners of the bathroom without any disinfectant and just
ends up smearing the grime around. Repetition has the
cleaner in hand but never actually gets down to scrubbing.
It never pushes the gospel into the corners. Instead, it just
waves the cleaner in the general direction of the grime. It
attempts to wield the gospel like a magic word, speaking it
like a mantra in the vicinity of a sin or a struggle in hopes
that something remarkable will happen. And because the
gospel is front and center, it has the appearance of avoiding

the problem of legalism, but it doesn't actually address the sin in question.

This often makes bare repetition the more subtle danger since it frequently goes undetected in churches that trumpet the good news about Jesus. Not only is it more subtle, but the long-term effects are just as destructive as legalism, since it gives the illusion of applying the gospel without actually doing so. A person who tries to wield the gospel like a mantra and finds it ineffective easily falls into despair. He thinks, *If not even the gospel can deliver me from the power of sin, then I must truly be hopeless.*

We need to be aware of these two dangers. Legalism is not the same as gospel obedience. Merely repeating the gospel is not the same as wisely applying it. Applying the gospel is bringing the weight of the good news to bear on a particular sin in such a way that the specifics of the gospel connect with the specifics of the sin at hand by the power of the Holy Spirit.

Applying the gospel starts with the gospel itself. It starts with the royal announcement that God has loved us so much that he has sent his only Son to die a sinner's death in our place and that Jesus Christ, the crucified and risen Messiah, is Lord of heaven and earth. By faith in him, we can be forgiven and cleansed of all of our sins, accepted by God, delivered from his wrath, adopted into his family, and built into the temple of his Holy Spirit. This is the gospel. We begin here, and we never outgrow it. We begin by the Holy Spirit, and we are perfected by the Holy Spirit.

We are saved by grace, and we live in grace. But growth in grace is the penetration of the gospel into every area of our heart, every recess of our mind, and every sphere of our life. Applying the gospel begins with a growing, experiential grasp of God's work in Christ.

But applying the gospel doesn't stop there. We must also have a deepening understanding of ourselves, our own particular temptations, our own besetting sins, our own burdens and weights, our own wounds and aches. We cannot rightly apply the gospel to ourselves until we mature in our own self-knowledge. We cannot rightly apply the gospel to others until we understand the nature of sin and temptation in general, as well as the anatomy of specific, identifiable sins for us. It does no good to say that "sin is in there somewhere" and that the gospel is the remedy for it. We must get specific, we must probe our past and present experiences, and we must examine our hearts. In short, we must learn to grow in experiential wisdom, in practical maturity.

> We cannot rightly apply the gospel to ourselves until we mature in our own self-knowledge.

Practically speaking, this means that when we apply the gospel, we will probably spend the bulk of our time talking about something other than the gospel. For example, after unpacking the glorious gospel of God's grace for three chapters in Ephesians, Paul does not seek to apply the gospel by simply repeating himself for three more. Instead, in Ephesians 4–6, he offers exhortations to godly behavior, commands to avoid sin, and experiential wisdom, interspersed with brief grounding statements that hearken back to gospel realities unpacked in earlier chapters. In other words, when Paul applies the gospel, he mostly talks about things besides the gospel. Or more accurately, he talks about other things through the lens of the gospel.

When he talks about these other things—whether pride or lust or envy or fear or singleness or marriage—the gospel's weighty presence is felt everywhere. The gospel is not what he is looking *at;* it's what he is looking *through.* This is what we must learn to do. We must be able to assume the gospel and talk about other things in such a way that the reality of the gospel is brought to bear on the problems and sins, even as it explicitly comes to the surface at key moments.

Finally, applying the gospel means we ultimately rely on God to bring the good news of King Jesus to bear on our lives. The Spirit is the life-giving bridge between the reality of the gospel and our own renewed conduct. Both justification and sanctification, both our position and our progress, are ultimately God's work.

A Word to Mentors

What About Romans 7?

Earlier, I noted that I used to think Galatians 5:16–17 was a synopsis or brief summary of Romans 7. I described how one of my classmates in seminary helped me understand Galatians more clearly. But what about Romans 7? Is this a description of the normal Christian life?

Many commentators and pastors view it that way. They think Paul is describing his own ongoing struggle with indwelling sin as a Christian. What's more, many Christians identify with the frustrations Paul describes; we all know what it feels like to be confused by our actions and to hate the things we do. Nevertheless, I don't think Romans 7 is describing the normal Christian life.

The main reason is that, aside from a brief mention in verse 6, the Spirit is completely absent from Romans 7; he doesn't show up until Romans 8. I can't imagine Paul discussing the normal Christian life without referring to the Holy Spirit, who is the ground and power beneath all our efforts. What's more, the person described in Romans 7 is "of the flesh, sold . . . under sin" (v. 14), which seems to run counter to Romans 6:7 and 6:14, where Paul says that we have been justified from sin and that we are no longer under the dominion of sin. Far from a person who has been set free from sin's dominion, the picture Paul presents in Romans 7 is of a long and frustrating defeat: I know what's right, and I want to do what's right, but I lack the ability to carry it out. In other words, I can't gratify my good desires because the sin that dwells in me is a powerful slave master. That doesn't sound like the kind of talk the Bible expects from a Christian.

In Romans, the real change comes in chapter 8—no condemnation in Christ and the arrival of the Spirit of life who liberates me from the law of sin and death so that I am now able to fulfill God's requirements as I walk according to the Spirit (vv. 1–4). Thus, my own view is that Romans 7 is a fitting description of an Old Testament believer (think of David in the Psalms), who delights in God's law but finds himself frustrated in his ability to overcome the flesh and its sinful desires because the Spirit is not yet poured out in his fullness (see Jer. 31; Ezek. 36; John 7:37–39). This is precisely what is suggested by the one mention of the Spirit in Romans 7:6. Paul is drawing a contrast between serving God in "the new way of the Spirit" as opposed to the old way of the "letter" of the law. The remainder of Romans 7 describes the frustration of serving in the old way of the letter, in which sinful passions are aroused by the law, but the law is unable to transform the heart. Romans 8 celebrates the new way of the Spirit. The arrival of Jesus changes our fundamental situation. We are now totally freed from condemnation. Through the death of Jesus in our place, God has done what the law could not do: condemn our sin without condemning us. God is now happy with us because the final sacrifice has been offered. We are righteous in his sight. And with God's approval now assured and the Spirit poured out in our hearts, we are able to put sin to death and walk as sons of God.

I don't think this means that the struggle described in Romans 7 is irrelevant for the Christian. But I do think it puts the struggle in its proper place. When a Christian doesn't walk by the Spirit, we feel much like the frustrated man in Romans 7. We feel the weight and power of indwelling sin, and we despair of ultimately relying on our own efforts to walk in holiness. But, if I'm right, this is not our destination, nor should we settle in as though Romans 7 is the normal Christian life. Instead, like in Galatians 5, we should move from the frustration and the war toward deliverance from indulging our fleshly desires. And we do this by daily walking by the Spirit.

Not everyone may be persuaded by my understanding of the passage. But even if you think Paul is describing his own Christian experience, it's important to emphasize that the man in Romans 7 is not walking according to the Spirit. He may delight in God's law and have some desires to do what is right, but the law of sin and death at work in his body confuses and frustrates him. Thus, either way, it's important that we not use Romans 7 as an excuse to settle in and make peace with our sin. Instead, we ought to move from the confusion and frustration of Romans 7 to the victory and glory of Romans 8, where we set our minds on the

Spirit, and walk according to the Spirit, and put to death the deeds of the body by the Spirit.

Practically speaking, this means that, as a mentor, you may use Romans 7 to help the men in your group see their own frustrations and failures. But you mustn't let them make peace with their frustrations and failures. Help them see that it's good the Bible so accurately describes our experience; it helps us know that we're not alone. God knows our frame. Then help them not get stuck there. Don't allow them to wallow in the frustration of Romans 7. Romans 8 is just around the corner, and while it still describes a fight, the Spirit is at work to put to death the deeds of the body so that we can have true life and peace.

2

Starve the Beast

When I initially meet with a guy or a group of guys about sexual sin, the first thing I want to determine is how serious they are about resisting.

There have been times when men have ended up in my office mainly because of feelings of guilt over a recent failure or because a wife or a mentor has pressured them to talk to me because of a pattern of failure. Either way–whether because of momentary guilt or because of external pressure–they don't really want to be there, and there's no way to help someone who doesn't really want help. If momentary guilt or external pressure is pushing them to meet with me, then they will be engaged just enough to make the guilt go away or to relieve the pressure. The reality is that someone has to have a deep and persistent desire for lasting change, or they won't get lasting change. They must effectively be fed up with themselves and, therefore, committed to a costly obedience. But many men pray like Augustine did when he was young: "O Lord, give me purity (but not yet)." The guilt and shame of sexual sin is enough to make them feel bad but not enough to motivate them to the kind of Spirit-wrought effort that will be necessary to break free.

Establishing Artificial Boundaries

So how do I determine whether someone is truly fed up or only feeling guilty in the moment? How do I know if they are serious about holiness or still praying "not yet"? My own experience has taught me to lead with a simple but drastic action to gauge their seriousness. And the action is one I truly believe is necessary for any other progress to happen. I call it "creating space by starving the beast."

The basic idea is to establish artificial boundaries in relation to sexual temptation. This makes it possible for the deeper issues of the heart to surface without gasoline constantly being poured on the fire. Most often it means identifying the access point for the temptation and completely removing it.

For example, say a man is addicted to Internet pornography. He regularly searches it out and masturbates. In this case, one of the first things I'll do is to establish an artificial boundary: no Internet use when you are by yourself. I view this as an *absolute* rule but not a *permanent* rule. In other words, these sorts of artificial boundaries are designed to be temporary. The hope is that at some point the technology can be restored without restrictions. But temporary may be a long time. Sometimes I'll put an initial date on it (like six months). But my first goal is to get them to agree to some kind of boundary like this. It might be "no Internet use by yourself"; it might be "delete your Facebook account"; it might be "no Netflix alone." If a smartphone is a common avenue for temptation and lust, then I'll urge them to get a dumb phone that lacks Internet access. It might be some combination of all of these.

In all of these cases, the goal is to take some deliberate action that signals, "I'm serious about fighting sin. I'm willing to inconvenience myself for the sake of my holiness."

Now at this point you might be thinking, *That's just not feasible for me. I need my computer or phone for work. Or, I work from home a lot when no one is around. Or, I regularly work at night after my wife is in bed.* I understand the complications. But I'm not deterred by them. And you shouldn't be either. Jesus said it was better to enter the kingdom of God without an eye or a hand than not to enter the kingdom of God at all. Life with a dumb phone seems far less inconvenient than life with one hand.

Instead of being deterred, you should brainstorm with others how to navigate these inconveniences. For example, if you need to check your e-mail and no one else is at home, drive to a coffee shop in order to do it. Same thing if you're working at night and your family is asleep. Perhaps instead of working at night, you need to wake up early and drive to the coffee shop. Or ask your wife to stay up late or get up early with you, doing whatever she needs to do while you work at the kitchen table. Yes, such measures are inconvenient. But you can't carry fire next to your chest and expect not to get burned. You can't walk on hot coals and have unscorched feet (Prov. 6:27–28). Too many men pray, "Lead me not into temptation," and continue to surf the Internet alone at 2:00 a.m. and watch steamy movies on Netflix. They keep fire in their pocket and act surprised when they get burned. They prefer the convenience of their technology to progress in their holiness. And so it's important for us to establish artificial boundaries around the technology that is often the means of temptation and sin.

> You can't carry fire next to your chest and expect not to get burned. You can't walk on hot coals and have unscorched feet.

Is This Legalism?

Occasionally I've had men respond to the artificial barriers by raising concerns about legalism. There's no Bible verse that says, "Stay off the Internet when you're alone," so am I not requiring something more than what God requires? Or they ask whether I'm treating technology as the root of the problem, as opposed to addressing the real issue, which is the sinful heart. Now, to these questions, I say, "Yes, the heart is the real issue; the beast is within. But technology is feeding the beast, which means we need to do something about technology in order to learn how to kill it." We begin by cutting off the food supply.

What's more, establishing firm rules about technology isn't legalism. Rather, it's a direct application of Jesus' words in Matthew 5:30, to which I alluded earlier: "If your right hand causes you to sin, cut it off and throw it away. For it is better that you lose one of the parts of your body than for your whole body to go into hell." Hands are good, just like computers and smartphones. But hands that cause you to sin endanger your soul and must be amputated. And so must our technology if it becomes a stumbling block. Establishing artificial boundaries is mainly about identifying which "hand" is causing you to sin and then cutting it off. And given the violence of Christ's imagery, staying off the Internet when you're alone, in the grand scheme of things, is an inconvenience at worst, and pales in comparison to the value of one's holiness.

Over the course of my ministry, I've found that this initial, simple, but inconvenient requirement is revealing. It separates those who are willing to take drastic measures from those who are playing games. In fact, given all the demands on my time, I tend not to spend it on men who aren't even willing to be inconvenienced in order to walk by the Spirit. If they don't want to create space by starving the beast, if they don't want to establish the artificial boundaries necessary to deal with the heart, then all I can do is warn them about the gravity of sin and pray that they wake up to their danger. If you practice such things, you will not inherit the kingdom of God. If you live according to the flesh, you will die. If you don't cut it off, you are in danger of hell.

I once read a sermon by Charles Spurgeon on Jeremiah 23:29: "Is not my word like fire . . . and like a hammer that pulverizes rock?" In it, Spurgeon asks what we should do if we encounter a stony heart. He answers, "Try the hammer!" And if it doesn't break on the first strike, hit it again. And again.

Habits of Accountability and Confession

I'm assuming that, if you're still reading this book, then you're willing to be inconvenienced for the sake of your holiness. You're willing to adjust your habits and establish artificial boundaries in order to create space to starve the beast. Once you've identified some initial boundaries, the next step is to establish some accountability. That's what your mentor and the men in your group are for.

Accountability works like this. First, clearly agree to the boundary: "I will not be on the Internet when I am alone." Next, if you cross the boundary, if you get on the Internet alone, you've broken your word and need to confess it to your mentor and the other men in your group, *even if you don't look at pornography.* This is important. Having given your word about the boundary, you sin if you fail to abide by it. And you should confess that sin, even when it doesn't lead to lust.

At this early stage accountability has two goals. First, we want to begin to retrain the conscience. That's why clarity about the artificial boundaries is so important. Most guys who are neck-deep in sexual sin have desensitized consciences. They tend to be numb and deadened by sin. So one of our goals is to reawaken the conscience so it becomes rightly tuned and sensitive. We want it to be triggered early; the moment you get on the Internet alone, you ought to think, *Oh no; I promised the guys I wouldn't do this. Now I need to confess my failure to them.*

And this is the second goal of accountability—building habits and patterns of honesty, trustworthiness, and confession. Habits of confession are incredibly important in the Christian life. But when it comes to sexual sin, confession is a place where it's easy to go wrong, especially if a man is married and confessing sin to his wife.

It's possible for a guilty man to confess to his wife out of a desire for absolution and cleansing. The guilt weighs him down until he unloads it on her, at which point he feels the great relief of what he thinks is a clean conscience. The problem is that a man like that is effectively treating his wife like God. He's going to her for the fundamental cleansing of his conscience. Not only is this unwise for him; it's unfair to her. She's not able to bear the weight of being God.

Here's the kind of scenario I have in mind. A married man in sexual sin decides to come clean. He confesses his sin to his wife. As a result, he feels two conflicting emotions. On the one hand, he feels the relief of no longer hiding his sin. His conscience, which had been afflicting him, no longer feels the burden of his sinful actions (at least in part). On the other hand, he feels sorrow and sadness because he's deeply hurt his wife. The challenge going forward is that those two emotional responses will be in tension with each other. He will want to confess to her in order to get the relief, but he also knows that the confession will hurt her. In this scenario, confessing sin is like throwing up: he feels relief afterward, but his wife is now covered in vomit.

It gets even more complicated if he develops a sensitive conscience and doesn't have a good understanding of how much detail to share. He can overconfess, giving a level of detail that sits in her mind long after he's forgotten it. His relief comes at the expense of her peace of mind. Recognizing this, he might seek to hold details back. But his sensitive conscience means he won't get the relief and, as a result, will appear jittery and anxious. That anxiety stokes his wife's (reasonable) fear of his unfaithfulness, and she asks, "Is there anything else?" Because he knows he could always give more detail, he again appears uncertain and anxious, which further compounds her fears. It's a vicious trap.

A Better Way

The way to avoid the trap is to get clear on the order and purposes of different stages of confession. Though this is certainly a matter of wisdom and personal application, in my experience a wise and healthy pattern of confession runs like this.

First, you must confess your sin to God. Forthright, honest, sincere, no minced words. This repentance and confession is what puts you right in the universe. Period. Your sin was ultimately against God, and therefore God must ultimately forgive you. "Against you—you alone—I have sinned and done this evil in your sight" (Ps. 51:4). "Who can forgive sins but God alone?" (Mark 2:7). This is the fundamental forgiveness we all need, and this forgiveness stabilizes us for any subsequent confession to other people.

Next, having repented and confessed your sin to God, you should then confess your sin to other men. This is a fruit of repenting to God. The aim is healing and holiness. "Confess your sins to one another and pray for one another, so that you may be healed" (James 5:16). This confession should also be sincere, forthright, sufficiently specific, with no minced words or euphemisms.

I mention euphemisms because they are a particular danger in this area. Because of our guilt and shame, we tend to use words that cloud what we actually did. We say, "I've been struggling lately," or "I failed again." We leave it ambiguous and unclear because we feel ashamed of what we've done. In my experience, "I've been struggling" basically means, "I've been losing badly and often." "I've been struggling" actually means "I've been surrendering." Or sometimes we'll say, "I fell into sin," implying that we accidentally stumbled into immorality. The truth is we didn't fall; we jumped.

The effect, however unintentional, is to minimize or sanitize what we've done. Truthfulness and accuracy are what we're after—specificity without being graphic. "I looked at Internet pornography. I masturbated. I looked lustfully at a woman." A simple principle is to use the biblical words for sins. We should call things what God calls them: fornication, sexual immorality, lust, homosexuality. Where there is no direct biblical word, we ought to aim to be as concrete and specific as possible without being graphic.[1]

Returning to confession, the main aim of confessing to other men is healing and holiness. But a secondary aim is wise counsel from them about what and how to confess the sin to your wife. Is this violation the sort that must be confessed to her? If so, what level of detail needs to be shared? Wise counsel from other men has a stabilizing effect and prevents the kind of reactive anxiety that further damages your marriage.

---

[1] G. K. Chesterton once said something to the effect that nine times out of ten, the coarse word is the word that condemns the sin, whereas the refined word is the one that excuses it.

Finally, having confessed and been forgiven by God, and having confessed to other men for the purposes of accountability, healing, and holiness, you should confess to your wife—not in order to be put right in the universe but in order to make things right with her. But notice some-thing—this confession is now coming from a place of divine acceptance and wise counsel. In other words, you're now confessing *out of* your acceptance before God rather than confessing in order to receive absolution from your wife. What's more, if she knows you've confessed fully to God and to other men, and if she trusts the wisdom, godliness, and counsel of those men, then, Lord willing, she won't want to demand an unhealthy disclosure of details that will cause more damage to the marriage. A man who is resting in God's approval and has been counseled by godly men is able to calmly and sorrowfully say to his wife, "This is what I've done. I've confessed it to God. I've confessed it to these men. And they counseled me to share this much detail with you. I'm so sorry that I've hurt you. And here are the steps we're taking to make sure it doesn't happen again."

Conclusion

So then, these are the initial practical steps in seeking to be free from sexual sin and pursue holiness. First, we establish simple, but inconvenient artificial boundaries around the technologies and areas that most often lead us to sin. We take concrete and drastic action in the fight. We identify the "hand" that is causing us to sin, and we cut it off. Not only does this communicate our seriousness in the fight against pornography and sexual sin; it also begins to create space for the coming heart work by cutting off lust's present food supply. The artificial barriers will reduce the opportunities for sinful indulgence so that we can begin to grow in self-control.

Second, having established these artificial boundaries, we seek others to hold us accountable to them. The goal of this accountability is twofold—we want to begin to retrain our consciences, and we want to develop healthy habits of confession. We want our consciences to alert us to danger, to keep us from sin, and to convict us when we fail. And we want to confess our sins to God for ultimate forgiveness, confess them to other men for healing and counsel, and then, when necessary, confess them to our wives for restoration and wholeness.

These two initial steps are crucial means in our battle for victory, freedom, and healing. But as we employ them, we must remember that we are to *use* means, not *trust in* means. Our trust is in the Lord. He must act in and through all of our efforts if the change is to be real and lasting. Our efforts are only glorifying to God when we're doing them in reliance on him, when we're seeking to walk *by the Spirit.*

A Word to Mentors

Web Filters and Computer Software

Whenever I talk about the creation of artificial boundaries, the question of Web filters and computer monitoring programs inevitably comes up. Men wonder, *Do I really need to get rid of my smartphone or agree to abstain from the Internet when I'm alone? Or can I simply install a Web filter or program like Covenant Eyes?*

In my own counseling and mentoring, I tend not to rely on these sorts of programs and technological barriers. This isn't because I think they have no value; I'm sure in some cases they may help create the space to starve the beast. However, my approach is built on an initial and temporary dose of hard medicine ("cut it off"), followed by a full restoration once internal self-control has been demonstrated over time. Monitoring programs and Web filters don't really fit this strategy.

For starters, such programs and filters are commonly used as a permanent strategy for avoiding sexual sin rather than a temporary barrier that's designed to create space for self-mastery under the Spirit's guidance. What's more, monitoring programs automatically expose attempts to seek out sexually explicit material and thus run the risk of short-circuiting the habits of voluntary confession and honesty. I want men to learn to willingly bring their sin into the light rather than have a computer program automatically send a report to an accountability partner or mentor. Additionally, the effectiveness of computer monitoring software is dependent on the mentor's ability to read and act on the automatic reports. If a mentor is attempting to help a group of men, then that's a significant time investment for him. It turns him into the policeman for the group, whose job is to monitor and punish infractions, rather than the father in the faith who calls the men to grow up into maturity.

Ultimately, I fear that automatic reports treat men like children, whereas requiring and expecting honest confession challenges them to take responsibility for themselves and their actions. At the same time, I should note that monitoring programs, Web filters, and Web blockers are great tools for a man to protect his children from pornography. Kids need that kind of external protection because of their vulnerability and immaturity. But with grown men, we're after something more. We want Spirit-wrought self-mastery and stability.

Now, my strategy means it is possible for men to hide and lie about their thoughts and actions. If they don't confess their sin, then you won't know about it. But I actually look at this as a strength of my approach. It's good for men to feel that their spiritual vitality depends on their own honesty, and not on a mentor's ability to police their behavior. And there are other, better ways to minimize the danger of someone persistently hiding his sin and failing to confess. One simple strategy is to pray regularly that God would bring hidden sin to light. For example, whenever you're meeting with a group of men, you might include something like this in your corporate prayer: "Father, your Word promises that nothing is hidden that will not be revealed. So if there is hidden and unconfessed sin among us, we ask that you bring it to light and expose it for the sake of our souls, our families, our church, and your mission in the world. May there be no Achans in the camp that compromise the holiness of your people (Josh. 7). What's more, Father, we ask that, whatever you have to do to make us holy, do it. Draw near to us so that we experience the reality of your holiness as good and life-giving, as you strip away all that would keep us from you and heal our brokenness."

That kind of prayer has two good effects. To begin, it places the ultimate burden for exposing sin on the God who sees all of our hearts and all of our actions: "No creature is hidden from [his sight], but all [of us] are naked and exposed to the eyes of him to whom we must give an account" (Heb. 4:13). Second, it reminds us that God is real and causes us to fear that he will answer such a prayer if we try to hide. We may be able to game the system and get around the computer monitoring and Web filters. But God is never fooled. Regular prayers for exposure remind us that our God is the living God, that he never slumbers or sleeps, and that he is so committed to our good that he will wreck us in order to make us holy.

If automatic reports run the risk of treating men like children, Web filters can treat them like wild beasts who are constantly testing the fences to see if they can escape. In fact, monitoring systems and Web filters can actually enflame desire by offering a beatable obstacle to sin. Gaming the system can become part of the thrill. (That was my experience in college.) In my mind, it's better and simpler just to cut it off.

What's more, part of the strength of my strategy ("no Internet by yourself") is the inconvenience and (minor) sacrifice. The cost (in terms of ease of access to the Web) is part of the benefit for the soul. Driving to the coffee shop to check an e-mail reminds us of the patterns of sin we are attempting to leave behind and reinforces our willingness to pursue holiness and put sin to death. Because the inconvenience is temporary, there is a concrete goal to shoot for: we want to be so in control of our impulses and actions that the external barriers can eventually be removed.

To put it succinctly, we want the external barriers to be a temporary crutch, not a permanent artificial leg. We want the boundaries to be internalized; we want the conscience to be recalibrated and sensitive to conviction; we want habits of confession and repentance to be woven into the lives of the men in our churches.

3

How Do Humans Work?

At this point we've done two things: we've laid a basic biblical foundation for the Christian life, and we've taken two initial steps in the fight against lust and pornography. Now we're almost ready to press on to the actual daily battleground.

Before we do this, it will be helpful to get some clarity on the battleground itself. This means understanding something about anthropology (the doctrine of man) and something about psychology (the doctrine of the soul). This chapter will give the broad strokes on each of these and then attempt to bring them together into a coherent picture of the mind and the body. Think of the next two chapters as surveying a map of the battlefield before the fighting actually begins.

Aspects of this chapter may feel complicated, so keep the goal in mind. We want to gain clarity about how we operate as human beings so we can grow in our ability to resist temptation and sin. In my experience, this kind of growth in self-knowledge is useful in breaking patterns of sin. Once I know there's a certain logic and rationale to my behavior, it's easier to interrupt the cycle.

Anthropology: What Is Man?

Let's begin with biblical anthropology. Here we're dealing with the basic question: What is man?

A human person is a unity of body and soul, with the soul as the animating principle of the body, breathed into us by God (Gen. 2:7). So deep is the union between body and soul that rupturing that union is called death (James 2:17). While our souls can survive the death of the body, the Bible makes clear that a bodiless existence is undesirable and alien to our nature (2 Cor. 5:4). God made us to be embodied beings, and even a soul cleansed of every trace of sin still longs to be reunited with the body in resurrection. This is the basic picture of human nature—we are embodied souls.

Classically, theologians have distinguished four states or stages of human nature—original, corrupted, redeemed, and glorified. In my own teaching I've found it useful to build on those stages by adding a fifth and linking each stage to a particular era in history. So here are the five stages or states of human nature:

1. Original State—in the Garden
2. Corrupted State—Exiled from Eden
3. Redeemed State—before Christ
4. Redeemed State—after Christ
5. Glorified State—New Creation

Let's walk through these one at a time.

First, there is our *original* state. This is human nature as God intended it when he created us. Our original nature was good and directed toward the purposes for which we were made.

Second, because of the fall and the entrance of sin, you and I never experience human nature in its original state. Instead, we have to deal with human nature in a *corrupted* state. This is human nature as it has been distorted by human sin and decay and death. This is what Paul refers to when he says that we are "by nature children under wrath" (Eph. 2:3). Our corrupt nature means that the tendencies and trajectories of our original nature have been derailed and disordered. They veer from their true purpose and, in doing so, become unnatural (Rom. 1:26–27).

But the fact that we're no longer in our original state doesn't mean the goodness of our nature has been totally abolished. Nature is stubborn, and even though it has been corrupted, we can still recognize God's imprint and handiwork despite the sin that mars us. This means, whenever we witness an act of our corrupt nature, we should ask, "What part of our original nature is under there? What good is being twisted by human brokenness and rebellion?" Because beneath our corruptions lies God's original good design.

Third, we can speak of human nature in its *redeemed* state but with an additional distinction between redemption prior to Christ and redemption after Christ. Human beings have always required the new birth in order to escape sin, corruption, and death. But it seems to me the Bible teaches that there's a difference between redemption in the old covenant, before Christ came and poured out the Spirit, and redemption in the new covenant. Believers in the Old Testament were born again; they were circumcised in heart. At the same time, because Christ had not fully and finally dealt with sin, the Spirit was not yet poured into their hearts in the way he is under the new covenant. The permanent indwelling of the Spirit is a new covenant blessing (Jer. 31; Ezek. 36). That means we experience a richer and fuller level of redemption than the saints in the Old Testament who looked forward to the coming of Christ (John 7:37–39; Heb. 11:39–40).[1]

So when it comes to human nature in its redeemed state, we distinguish old covenant and new covenant redemption. But even in the new covenant, redemption is

---

[1] If you're interested in chasing down this distinction, James M. Hamilton Jr.'s book, *God's Indwelling Presence: The Holy Spirit in the Old and New Testaments* (Nashville: B&H Academic, 2006) explores the movement from old covenant to new covenant in some detail.

not yet complete. Aspects of our corruption still remain; we are still "in the flesh." But we are not dominated by our sin and corruption as we were. Grace has changed us and begun a restoration project. The present incomplete restoration is the down payment of our future inheritance when God fully and finally transforms us. This is human nature in its *glorified* state, when the whole person, body and soul, is entirely delivered from sin and death and decay, and we attain God's original purposes for human beings.

Original state. Corrupted state. Redeemed state before Christ. Redeemed state after Christ. Glorified state. These are the five basic states of human nature throughout history.

Psychology: How Do We Experience the World?

When we turn to psychology, we are asking questions about how we, as embodied souls, experience the world. How do we live and move and have our being in the world God has made? In answering that question, it's helpful to think in terms of different levels.

At the bottom, certain aspects of our existence operate automatically and apart from any rationality or choice. Breathing, digesting food, pumping blood, growing—our bodies do these things automatically without any reasoning or decision on our part. These processes are beautifully designed but completely subrational, and we share them with all forms of life, whether plants or animals.

At the other end of the spectrum, at the highest level, we can speak of *the mind*, which includes the intellect—the faculty by which we think and judge and reason—and the will—the faculty by which we desire, love, hate, and choose something. This is the level of rational and moral agency, and it is one of the things that makes us like God and angels.

Often this is as far as we get—higher rational faculties in the mind, lower subrational processes in the body. But both the Bible and our experience suggest that we should add an additional middle level. The middle level has characteristics of each of the other levels. On the one hand, the middle level is tightly linked to the senses of the body and operates immediately and intuitively. On the other hand, this middle level has a kind of rationality and logic to it. Like the mind, we can divide it into a perceiving power and a desiring power, into a power that observes, recognizes, and identifies something, and a power that likes or dislikes, desires, or rejects the thing. Medieval Christians referred to this middle level as "sense apprehension" and "sense appetite."

One way to understand this middle level is to think of it as the aspect of our nature we share with other animals. A rabbit is not a moral agent. It lacks the higher faculties of intellect and will. It doesn't reason or choose the way we do. In short, rabbits aren't persons. At the same time, a rabbit isn't just a bundle of automatic processes. Rabbits can perceive and respond to the world. When a rabbit sees a wolf, it immediately recognizes what the wolf is and intuitively reacts to the wolf's presence by running away and hiding. This isn't reasoning and choosing like the human mind does, nor is it a subrational automatic process like breathing. It's somewhere in between. There's a good reason the rabbit is running, but the rabbit didn't reason and then make a decision as a person would. It acted intuitively and instinctively.

The Rider and the Elephant

I think it's important to recognize the place of this "middle level." Matthew LaPine is a contemporary author who has helped me understand and appreciate these categories. He refers to this view of the human person as a "tiered psychology," since we can speak of higher faculties (intellect and will, which operate according to rational and intentional processes) and lower faculties (sense apprehension and sense appetite, which operate intuitively and almost automatically but with a rationality and logic of their own). According to LaPine, this type of tiered psychology enables us to explain the internal psychological conflict we all experience on a daily basis.

Borrowing an image from the social psychologist Jonathan Haidt, LaPine describes the relationship between the higher faculties and the lower faculties as a rider attempting to steer an elephant. The higher faculties are the rider, which attempts to direct the elephant, representing the lower but powerful faculties. The internal conflict we experience is basically the attempt of the rider to tame and steer an unruly elephant.

This image basically tracks with the distinction the Bible draws between the mind and the body (or the flesh). When the biblical authors talk about the body and the flesh in moral terms, they're not talking about subrational automatic processes like digestion and breathing. They're talking about the lower level of desires, appetites, and passions. They're talking about the elephant.

It's important to stress that the elephant, while powerful, can be trained and conditioned. The body, with its intuitions and appetites, is both malleable and stubborn; it can both be shaped and afterward hold its shape. That is, we can develop habits, whether for good or ill. While our mind and body were both created good, since the fall, our corruption extends to the whole person, both mind and body. As Paul says in Ephesians 2, in our natural, corrupt state, we are all under the dominion of sin and the devil. We follow the course of this world. We live "in our fleshly desires, carrying out the inclinations of our flesh *and* thoughts" (v. 3; emphasis added). Notice that both the mind and the flesh have desires; the flesh is not subrational but has appetites and passions of its own.

In Romans 6–7, Paul explains more clearly what he means by "living in the flesh." He refers to the "body ruled by sin" by which we are "enslaved to sin" (Rom. 6:6). In fact, that's a good definition of *flesh*: "the body and its desires, under the power and dominion of sin and the curse." As he says in Romans 6:12, in our corrupt state sin reigns in our bodies so that we obey its passions. People who live in the flesh have their sinful passions aroused by the law so that these passions are working and active in the members of the body, leading to death. As he describes the internal conflict of the soul, he notes that evil and sin dwell "in me" (Rom. 7:17). They enslave him (Rom. 7:14) and hold him captive (Rom. 7:23). The picture is one in which the higher faculties are dominated by the lower faculties and passions under the dominion of sin.

Earlier I said that I think the frustration of the man in Romans 7 reflects the condition of a believer under the old covenant, one who agrees with God's holy law about what is good and right but is frustrated in his attempts to carry it out. We can now fill out this picture by identifying the source of this frustration. The trouble for this old covenant saint is that, while he has been born again and given a new heart, his flesh is still habituated and dominated by sin. He knows what's right, but he can't do it. (In saying this, I'm not suggesting that Old Testament saints never obeyed God; they clearly did.) To use the image from earlier, he is attempting to ride an unruly and untamed elephant, which frustrates his desires to steer in the right direction. The elephant's destructive impulses (the corrupt passions of the flesh) overwhelm his efforts to live in harmony with God and his law.

What changes then after the coming of Christ and the pouring out of the Spirit? When God gives us the fullness of his Spirit in the new covenant, he shifts the balance of power in the conflict between the higher faculties, which are now governed by the Spirit, and the lower powers (or the flesh), which still retain the old desires and habits. This accounts for the warfare in Galatians 5, which I mentioned in the first chapter. The desires of the Spirit are desires of the higher faculties under the influence of God's Spirit, which are now opposed to the desires of the flesh (or the lower faculties). The elephant is still unruly, but the rider is now strengthened and renewed by the almighty Spirit of the living God, and in walking by the Spirit he is able to tame and train the elephant.

Putting the Pieces Together

Now there's much more to be said on the subject. This is just the broad outline of the picture. For now, let me briefly pull together the anthropology and the psychology so that we can have a better understanding of the place where the battle with sin takes place. Here are the five states of human nature and the interactions between the different levels of the human psyche.

1. **In our original state everything is good.** The higher faculties of the mind rule the lower faculties and passions, and because we have access to the tree of life, the automatic processes of the body sustain the life of man indefinitely. The soul animates the body and all parts of the human person cohere and operate properly. Rider and elephant work together in perfect harmony.

2. **After the fall, every aspect of our nature is corrupted.** The union between soul and body begins to dissolve, eventually leading to their separation at death. The automatic processes of the body still work but are plagued by disease, pain, and dysfunction. Both the higher and lower faculties (the mind and the body) are under the dominion and power of sin. The desires of the flesh dominate us, as our bodies are habituated to sin and the curse, and our minds follow the lead of the lower faculties, willfully following the course of this world and the devil. Both rider and elephant are in rebellion against God.

3. **Under the old covenant, the saints are born again through the promises of God.** They delight in God's law with the higher faculties of their minds; they desire to do the right thing. However, the passions of the flesh are still powerful and frustrate many of their attempts at obedience. Sin dwells in their members and bears fruit for death. The rider may agree with God and his law, but the elephant is so strong that he frequently lives in the frustration of what is at best a stalemate, crying out for deliverance from the body of death.

4. **In the new covenant, the saints are not only born again through the living and abiding Word of God, but they are also indwelled and empowered by the Spirit of the living God.** The Spirit of Jesus himself abides in us and sets us free from the law of sin and death, enabling us to put to death the deeds of the body and to resist gratifying the desires of the flesh. There is still internal conflict. The desires of the flesh still war against the desires of the Spirit. The elephant is still unruly and habituated to sin. But the rider is strengthened

by grace and by that grace is able to begin to tame and train the elephant. Our transformation will only be imperfect in this life. Nevertheless, it is real and true as we walk by the Spirit and grow in the grace and knowledge of the Lord Jesus.

5. **We now await the new creation.** Then the desires of the flesh will be fully restored and reordered. Corrupt desires will be completely removed. Body and soul will be reunited in perfect harmony, and the whole person, mind and body, will be rightly oriented to God.

So much for the big picture. The next chapter will describe some of the effects of pornography on both the body and the mind.

A Word to Mentors

Justification, Sanctification, and Union with Christ

In laying the biblical foundation in these first few chapters, I've tried to make the concepts as accessible as possible. However, it's worth noting that the difference between "position" and "progress" (from chapter 1) is roughly the same as what theologians often mean by "justification" and "sanctification." Traditionally, justification refers to the decisive moment when we are set right with God, and sanctification refers to the ongoing growth in holiness over the course of our lives. I think it's fine to use those terms that way since it's a common historical way of describing the Christian life.

My own reason for not using these terms is that there are both positional and progressive aspects to righteousness and holiness. The Bible describes justification (or God declaring us righteous) as a definitive act at the beginning of the Christian life: "There is now no condemnation for those [who are] in Christ" (Rom. 8:1); we are justified by faith and therefore have peace with God (Rom. 5:1). But the Bible also urges us to walk in righteousness and to live righteous lives. (The English words *justification* and *righteousness* are both translating Greek words with the same basic root meaning; the word *justification* comes into English through Latin, whereas *righteousness* comes into English through Anglo-Saxon. But they're both translating words with the Greek root *dik-*. The same is true of *sanctification* (Latin) and *holiness* (Anglo-Saxon), which both come from the Greek root *hagi-*. Paul speaks of our sanctification in the past tense (1 Cor. 6:11), and the biblical authors urge us to strive for holiness (Heb. 12:14). In both cases there's a positional aspect, followed by an ongoing or progressive aspect. Here's my way of putting the various images of salvation in Scripture together into a coherent whole.

When God saves us, the fundamental thing he does is unite us to Christ by faith. Union with the crucified and risen Lord Jesus is what salvation fundamentally *is*. But in order to help us understand the wonder and glory of our union with Christ, God gives us multiple word pictures or metaphors to reveal the significance of what Christ has done for us. We can unpack union with Christ in terms of a law court. We are guilty and stand condemned, but Christ lives, dies, and is raised on our behalf, and, therefore, God declares us righteous in him. As a result, we leave the courtroom and seek to live upright and godly lives. Or we can unpack union with Christ using imagery from the temple. God is holy and, therefore, cleanses impure things and sets apart common things for holy use. There is a decisive cleansing and sanctifying work when we trust in Christ, and then the rest of our lives is an attempt to live holy lives, set apart from sin and evil. We can do the same with a family metaphor. God causes us to be born again, and then we seek to walk faithfully as his children. Or he adopts us into his family (that's conversion), and we now walk as obedient sons. So also with the image of slavery and redemption. We were enslaved to sin and death, and God decisively liberates us when he unites us to his Son. From then on we seek to live as free men, since it is for freedom that Christ has set us free. The same holds true for salvation: God delivers us from the *penalty* of sin (death) and then throughout our lives increasingly rescues us from the *power* of sin, all in anticipation of the day when we'll be completely delivered from the *presence* of sin. In each case, faith in Christ leads to a new *position* before God, and that new position leads to ongoing *progress* in conforming our lives to our new reality.

When it comes to exploring the fuller theological picture, I'd encourage you to use wisdom in knowing when and how much to dive deeper. The men you are seeking to help to grow in godliness and maturity don't need to fully "get" the heavy-duty theology in order to begin making progress. In fact, at this point, many of them only need the bare bones: we are sinners, Christ is our Savior, and God is fundamentally and decisively for us and has given us the Holy Spirit to enable us to walk in a manner worthy of the gospel. They can start there; they don't have to get the full ins and outs at the beginning.

However, it is important that *you* get it, as the one seeking to lead them, even as their growth in knowledge and
understanding only comes with time. We pastors often
think people first need to get the theory right, and then
they can put it into practice. That's because pastors tend
to love thinking theoretically. And some of your men will
eagerly digest the theory and then attempt to live it out suc-
cessfully. But I've often found that clarity at the theoretical
level comes from sincere attempts to obey at the practical
level. When I attempt to put the little bits that I do know
into practice, I find that I internalize God's work in my life,
and the paradigm becomes clear. As George MacDonald
once said, "Obedience is the opener of eyes."

As you meet with your men, I recommend giving some
brief instruction on the broader paradigm for change, but
don't get bogged down in the theology. Instead, get to work
at the practical level. I suspect your men will learn the
appropriate categories and distinctions as they are guided
in their use by a wise teacher. Your grasp of the deep biblical roots beneath the surface of your exhortations and
guidance will be felt in your counsel, and there will be
plenty of opportunities for those fundamental principles
to emerge as you go along.

4

Presenting the Body and Renewing the Mind

In the last chapter I mentioned Matthew LaPine, who has helped me appreciate the tiered psychology in the Bible. In one place LaPine notes that Paul gives two primary exhortations in Romans 6, one directed at the mind and one directed at the body. Paul says, "Consider yourselves dead to sin and alive to God in Christ Jesus" (v. 11), and "offer . . . all the parts of yourselves to God as weapons for righteousness" (v. 13). In other words, in our sanctification, there's a mental dimension (*"Consider yourself* in a certain way") and a bodily dimension (*"Present your members* to a certain power"). We need to "take every thought captive" (2 Cor. 10:5), and we need to pummel our bodies and make them our slaves (see 1 Cor. 9:27). The same two dimensions appear later in Romans 12, where we're exhorted to *present our bodies* as a living sacrifice and to be transformed by the *renewing of our minds* (vv. 1–2). In this chapter I'd like to explore these two dimensions of sexual sin (and pornography, in particular).

How Porn Weaponizes the Body

Romans 6 gives an amazing description of sin's effect on the body. Sin reigns in the body, making us obey its passions (6:12). We can present our members (that is, our body parts) to sin as instruments of unrighteousness (6:13). This presentation of our body parts to sin has a compounding effect: offering them as slaves to impurity and lawlessness leads to more impurity and lawlessness (6:19). Sin begets more and deeper sin.

Nowhere is this more clear than in the use of pornography. Porn use effectively weaponizes the body. By habituating the body to sin, it turns the body into an enemy. Our bodies become tools, instruments in the hands of sin and unrighteousness. Sin becomes our slave master, and we feel as though we are debtors to the flesh and, therefore, *must* live according to the flesh (Rom. 8:12).

The latest neuroscience on porn use confirms the Bible's description. If you'd like to do a deep dive on the bodily dimension, I've included some references at the end of the book. For now, I'll just offer a brief summary.

Essentially, pornography rewires the brain. The brain is what scientists call "plastic"; it's capable of being shaped and molded, and then of holding that new shape over time.

Brain plasticity is particularly high during one's teenage years; as we age, our brains become less malleable. Given that many men first encounter porn as teenagers, it's no surprise that they become hooked and find it difficult to break the habit as they get older. Porn weaponizes the brain so that sin is easy, and obedience is hard.

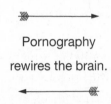

Pornography rewires the brain.

Looking at pornography triggers neurological, chemical, and hormonal events that leave a mark on the brain. Frequent use hardens the neural pathways and molds the brain so that it craves porn. Of course, this isn't unique to porn. Alcohol, drugs, video games, smartphones, food—all of these can do the same. But porn is somewhat unique in that it is a poly-drug, meaning it is both an upper (a dopamine high like cocaine) and a downer (an opiate release like heroin). I won't go into all of the details; check the articles in the appendix for more. But it is useful to see how the porn high that builds up to orgasm and then the porn crash that occurs afterward is a potent and addictive drug.

The upper is caused primarily by dopamine, which is released when we see sexual images and become aroused. Novelty triggers excess dopamine, which is why many men don't move straight to the pursuit of an orgasm but instead linger and search for image after image after image. A kind of "arousal addiction" sets in as guys hunt for the perfect

image. It's basically the pornographic counterpart to foreplay prior to sexual intimacy. With each new image the
dopamine spikes.[1]

The downer of porn is primarily caused by opiates
released through orgasm. It's why we feel tired and relaxed
after sex. But these opiates, along with the release of nor-
epinephrine prior to orgasm, also have another effect: these
chemicals and hormones are responsible for storing the
memory of what caused the euphoric sensation. Basically,
they take a neurological snapshot of what was happening
when the pleasurable sensation occurred. In doing so, they
bind us to the object that triggers the orgasm.

Now it's not difficult to see God's purposes for this sort
of mechanism. Sex is designed as the consummation of the
one-flesh union between husband and wife. God intends
for that neurological snapshot to be taken as a husband
makes love to his wife so that the two of them are more
tightly bound together. Orgasms are meant to strengthen
the bonds of marriage.

But compare the different snapshots that are taken
when a man makes love to his wife and when a man looks
at pornography. In the former you have the presence of

---

[1] Scientists have identified a phenomenon called the
"Coolidge effect," in which male mammals (including humans)
have renewed sexual interest when new sexual partners are
introduced. Pornography basically provides endless new sexual
"partners" and thus fosters endless dopamine hits and arousal
addiction.

the wife. It's a holistic experience engaging all five senses. There's an emotional connection between them. There might have been a date earlier. The brain remembers these circumstances as the occasion for the pleasure of the orgasm. Conversely, when a man looks at porn, he's alone in the dark. He's a voyeur, watching other people engage in sexual activity. He's clicking a mouse or typing on a computer or touching a screen. There's no emotional connection with another human being. So, when he has an orgasm, his brain remembers "computer, dark, alone, scrolling, swiping."

The effect of this is to habituate a man to be drawn to porn whenever he finds himself in the similar circumstances. When he sits down at his computer alone in the dark, even if he has no intention of looking for pornography, the elephant gets restless. Like Pavlov's dog, it's been conditioned to respond to certain stimuli. Conversely, a man who has trained his body for porn may find it difficult to become and stay aroused when engaging with his wife. She doesn't provide the endless novelty to which he's conditioned himself. And so sin becomes easy, and real relationships become hard.

All of this is bad enough. But then you add in the law of diminishing returns. Novelty inevitably wears off, so a man must find greater novelty, which eventually means greater corruption and perversion in order to attain the dopamine kick. C. S. Lewis describes this as "an ever increasing craving for an ever diminishing pleasure."[2] That's why men tend to progress from soft-core pornography to hard-core pornography to a myriad of increasingly perverse forms of sexuality. Exacerbating all of this are the three deadly *A*s of modern pornography: affordability, accessibility, and anonymity.

Sexual sin has always been around. In the ancient world a man could visit a brothel or a temple prostitute in order to pursue immorality. Sixty years ago a man who wanted to look at porn could go to a store and purchase a magazine with a limited number of images from another human being (whose eyes he might try to avoid). But today there is an endless supply of images and videos in everyone's pocket, and accessing it requires no human interaction at all. The modern porn problem is unusual because of its ability to deliver unending novelty, anywhere, with total (apparent) anonymity. Given these factors, it's no wonder pornography is so addictive in the modern world.

And its consequences are devastating.

From porn-induced erectile dysfunction that robs us of marital intimacy to the overwhelming shame and horror caused by the increasing corruption of pornographic images, from the isolation and loneliness birthed from our sense of shame to the apathy and acedia that numbs us to the beauty and goodness of the world, culminating in a

---

[2] C. S. Lewis, *The Screwtape Letters*, chapter 9.

sense of hopelessness about the future–the devastation is real and unmistakable.

Here's the bottom line: porn use creates brain ruts, hardening the neural pathways and conditioning the body to make porn use easy and obedience hard. Our bodies become instruments of unrighteousness and impurity. Many men have had decades of habituation in porn use, going back to their formative years as children and teenagers. Their elephants have developed a taste for the endless novelty of porn, and their riders have begun to grow disillusioned and despairing of any possibility of change.

One last comment: everything I've said is meant as an explanation for why pornography is so addictive and difficult to overcome. But explanations are *not* excuses. Neuroscience can help *explain* sin, but it can never *excuse* sin. Explanations should produce compassion in us (especially for those who were exposed to pornography at a young age or whose pornography use came about as a result of sexual abuse or trauma). Explanations can also create patience in us, since we recognize how difficult it is to steer unruly elephants. At the same, as you consider the various layers of your own struggle, beware of the temptation to absolve yourself of responsibility. For most of us, our choices have weaponized our bodies and turned them into enemies. We may be in a pit, but we're the ones who dug it.

More important, however, understanding the bodily dimension of the struggle can also give us hope.

Pornography rewires the brain. But, as we'll see in the coming chapters, by the grace of God, it's possible to wire it back again.

Renewing the Mind

A weaponized body is only one side of the equation. Porn use doesn't just affect the body; it also corrupts the mind. The trajectory of sin in Romans 1 is that God gives us up to the lusts of the heart, to dishonorable passions, and to a debased mind. Paul echoes that sentiment in Ephesians 4, where he describes unbelieving Gentiles as those who walk in the futility of their minds, who are darkened in their understanding, alienated from the divine life, and ignorant because of their hard hearts (vv. 17–18). He then reminds his readers of what it means to follow Christ—that they have put off the old man with his corrupt and deceitful desires and instead have put on the new man and are being renewed in the spirit of their minds (vv. 20–24).

Pornography rewires the brain. But, by the grace of God, it's possible to wire it back again.

When it comes to sexual sin, we become especially skewed in our view of men, women, and sex. So a significant part of being renewed in the spirit of our minds is learning to view these three fundamental realities rightly.

Men and Women in the Image of God

Men and women are made in God's image. We reflect God and represent him in the world. Being made in God's image means we have a particular calling or vocation in the world. In Genesis 1:28, God gives humanity a mission: be fruitful, multiply, fill the earth, subdue it, and exercise dominion over its inhabitants.

God divides the human race into male and female in order to better accomplish this mission. This is our fundamental identity in creation—we are sons and daughters of God, bearing his image. This fundamental identity means that both men and women have incredible dignity and worth. Like God and the angels, we are persons, made to know ourselves and others and ultimately to know our Creator.

While both men and women bear God's image and are called to God's mission, we fulfill that mission in distinct ways, ways that are fitting for us as men and women. There's an asymmetry, a complementarity, between men and women. We are both different *from* each other and different *for* each other. The Bible instructs us in these differences by telling the story of how God made us in Genesis 1 and 2. This story shapes the way we should view ourselves as men and women, and later biblical authors confirm that this story has abiding significance for how we live today.

So what do we learn in Genesis 1–2 (and in the later parts of the Bible that build on it)? We learn that men and women are incomplete without each other, unable to fulfill the mission by ourselves; it's not good for man to be alone (Gen. 2:18). We learn that Adam was formed first, and then Eve, making him the head of his wife. We learn that the woman was made *out of* the man, as God builds her from Adam's rib. We learn that the woman was made *for* the man in a way that the man was not made *for* the woman (1 Cor. 11:9). Finally, we learn that man and woman are mutually dependent; the woman was made from man, but now every man is born of a woman (1 Cor. 11:12).

This means that men need to be reminded of their God-given headship and of the call to exercise it faithfully. While every man is not the head of every woman, man is the head of woman. This headship takes various forms in various relationships, sometimes in a formal relationship like marriage and other times in the vast array of informal relationships between men and women. Faithful headship means that men provide stability, provision, and protection as we fulfill God's mission together. Men should take initiative, should guard and protect those in their care, instructing them in the ways of God. Answering to this, woman is described as a suitable helper for man, assisting him in their shared divine calling. In marriage, while the husband is the head, God designed a wife to influence her husband for good, providing wisdom and counsel and inspiration to him, even as she gladly submits to his authority. Woman is the glory of man, his crown and brightness, and his strength is designed to help her shine. The biblical picture always reminds me of ballroom dancing at a wedding. In the dance the man leads, and his wife follows. He gently and carefully guides her around the floor. Nevertheless, all eyes are on her. She is the glory of the dance.

Now in Genesis, God divides the human race into man and woman in order to reunite them. Woman is taken out of man, and then brought to the man so that they can become one flesh. Sex is the consummation of this union and is designed for fruitfulness. The fruitfulness begins with the couple together as they grow in knowledge of each other. The common biblical euphemism for sexual union is "knowing." Adam *knew* his wife. Sex is about knowing and being known. Sex binds husband and wife together and then bears fruit, first in children, which are the fruit of the womb and the glory of the marriage, and then in producing households, and then societies, and then civilizations. Marital intimacy and procreation are the good and proper goals of sex.

How Porn Corrupts Our View of Men, Women, and Sex

Now that picture of men, women, and sex is completely out of step with the pattern of this world. And pornography conforms us to the pattern of this world.

Instead of seeing women as persons, helpers, glory, and, image bearers, pornography presents women as objects of consumption and degradation. Instead of making men into persons, protectors, providers, and image bearers, pornography turns men into beasts that devour. It sets us on a quest for false intimacy, as persons who were meant to be united in the bonds of marriage, family, and society are instead isolated from each other in cocoons of selfish and corrupt pleasure.

Every woman participating in pornography is being used, exploited, and abused. In a sense, then, pornography is socially acceptable sexual abuse. If you saw a woman in a back alley being sexually abused, you wouldn't stop and lust. If you recoil at that notion, ask yourself why putting a screen between you and the exploitation makes it any better? Wicked and evil men are taking her glory and dragging it through the mud, and in chasing it, you both further exploit her and dehumanize yourself.

All of that is aside from the undeniable fact that many of those engaged in the pornography you are tempted to consume are victims of sex trafficking. Even a woman who willingly participates is doing so because she's believing lies or is so broken that she numbs her pain through sexual exploitation. Central to renewing our minds is reminding ourselves again and again that men are not beasts and women are not objects. We are persons made in God's image who are called to abounding fruitfulness. And pornography is inherently fruitless and barren.

But tragically, it's a barrenness that spreads. Men who are addicted to porn begin to see every woman through a pornographic lens. Porn use doesn't stay isolated; it affects other relationships, including the relationship between husband and wife. A pastor friend of mine once wrote that pornography is sex ed curriculum put together by liars and incompetents. The marriage bed is to be undefiled, and Paul exhorts the Thessalonians to abstain from sexual immorality and to learn to control one's own body in holiness and honor, not in the passion of lust like the Gentiles who don't know God (1 Thess. 4:4–5). This means we shouldn't be catechized by pornography. But sadly, too many men are, and they bring that catechism to the marriage bed. Pornography shapes their desires and tastes.

Many young men enter marriage with false expectations created by pornography. They think women are just men with female bodies and that women desire sex in the same way as men. In fact, they think women desire sex in the way that corrupt and godless men desire it. They enter marriage with corrupt expectations and then think their wives are the ones with the problem when they won't go along with whatever folly their catechism taught them. They find that in order to become aroused, they must mentally jump back and forth between the wife in front of them and the pornographic fantasies stored in their memory. Some settle in and accept this. Others crumble in shame as they discover that getting married didn't fix their porn problem. If anything, by involving another real person, the porn problem becomes even more devastating.

And that's before considering the effects on children in the home. In fact, if you want to read a heartbreaking and sobering reflection on the devastation of pornography, look up a poem called "I Looked for Love in Your Eyes." Tim Challies posted it a few years ago after he wrote his book on sexual sin. In the poem a woman movingly describes her anguish as she comes face-to-face with her husband's addiction and the way it has deadened him inside. He doesn't make love to her; he makes hate to her. And it dooms intimacy between them. And that's not the worst of it. I can't help but weep when she describes her feelings when her young sons discover the images on their dad's computer.

This chapter was sobering to write. I suspect it was sobering to read. And much more could certainly be written about the effects and devastation of pornography on our bodies, our minds, and our relationships. When we consider how our bodies have been weaponized and our brains hijacked, when we consider how porn teaches us to view women as objects of consumption and turns us into guilt-ridden beasts that devour image after image, covering God's good gift of sexual intimacy with layers of shame, when we feel the weight of porn's affordability, accessibility, and anonymity, it's easy to feel hopeless and overwhelmed. So at this point, I want to say to you as clearly as I can: *there is hope.*

Jesus is real, and he is mighty to save. God's call to you is to consider yourself dead to sin and alive to God, to be transformed by the renewing of your mind, and to present your body parts to God as tools of righteousness. He has given you his Spirit to make all of that possible.

You now have a basic understanding of the Christian life. Position, then progress. Life, then lifestyle. Conversion, then conduct. And you've taken some initial steps to create space by starving the beast. Your artificial boundaries are there, and, Lord willing, you're beginning to develop healthy habits of confession to God, to men, and to your spouse (if you have one). And now you have a basic map of the battlefield—your body and your mind which have been wracked and wrecked by sin. The next step is to explore the nature of the war itself and to begin to fight.

A Word to Mentors

Gospel Presence

Learning to walk by the Spirit is a matter of having the right foundation, the right environment, and the right strategies. As a mentor and leader, you obviously have a role to play in cultivating all of them. However, you have a special role to play in creating the right environment for growth and progress, one that avoids the hopelessness that so often marks this struggle. In my experience, the fundamental factor in creating the right environment for intentional action, real accountability, and healthy habits of confession is your presence and demeanor as the pastor, mentor, or counselor. I call this "gospel presence."

By *gospel*, I simply mean the good news that as sinners we are embraced and accepted by God because of what Jesus has done for us. He lived the life we couldn't live. He died the death we should have died. And God raised him from the dead, triumphing over sin and death. Outside of Jesus there is no hope. In Jesus we have a living hope.

By *presence*, I mean there's a way of being, an orientation to life and reality and others, a fundamental attitude that emanates from the core of who you are that shapes and colors everything you do. The way you carry yourself. The aura you display. The impression you give. That's what

I mean by presence. And gospel presence is crucial for creating the right environment for dealing with any sin, and especially sexual sin.

Because gospel presence is more about the way someone carries himself than following a specific set of actions, it's difficult to define. However, I've found Colossians 3:1–17 to be a fruitful place to get the feel of it. Here are six aspects of "gospel presence" in the passage.

1. Gospel presence begins with setting one's mind on Christ (Col. 3:1–2). Set your mind. Set your affection. Orient your life by Christ, who is your life. He's the sun; everything in your life orbits around him.

2. Gospel presence means putting on the new self, or the new man (Col. 3:9–10). The fundamental contrast is between the old man (Adam) who rebelled against God, and the new Man (Jesus) who fully trusted, obeyed, and imaged God. Gospel presence means you "put on" the new Man, that you "clothe" yourself with Jesus. And that's a good image for it: you must wear Jesus like a cloak. Certain practices flow out of this presence. There is an old man with his practices, and a new man with his practices.

84

There are practices that come from and accord with sinful Adam and practices that come from and accord with Christ. You can't do the practice if you don't put on the presence.

3. Gospel presence means you are fundamentally defined by God's love in the gospel. "As God's chosen ones, *holy and dearly loved*, put on . . ." (Col. 3:12, emphasis added). There are characteristics and qualities you put on and practice because you are holy and beloved by God. He defines you: "By the grace of God I am what I am" (1 Cor. 15:10). His grace is what makes you who and what you are. Gospel presence means his love and grace define you, and you know it deep in your bones.

4. Gospel presence means you are ruled by the peace of Christ (Col. 3:15). You are firm, stable, steadfast, unshaken. You're not tossed to and fro. When storms come, you're planted on a rock. When chaos erupts, God's peace still reigns in your heart. A kind of stability and security comes from knowing you're loved by God, defined by grace, oriented by Christ, clothed with the new man.

5. Gospel presence means that the word of Christ dwells in you richly in all wisdom (Col. 3:16). Not just that you read your Bible, but that there is a richness and fullness and potency to the Word in your life. The Spirit of God hangs on you, and people around you feel that "here's a person who has been with God." Gospel presence means you have the wisdom to connect the Word of God to life in a way that bears fruit.

6. Gospel presence means all of your practices are done "in the name of the Lord Jesus" (Col. 3:17). Your actions bear his name; they testify to him and point to him and draw attention to him.

In future chapters I'll say more about the importance of your gospel presence. For now, I simply want to stress that your own resting and hoping in the gospel are crucial in helping others resist their own hopelessness and despair.

5

The Longer War

In the next few chapters, I want to get down to brass tacks by offering some reflections on the nature of the battle with sexual sin itself. Clarity on this is crucial for your fight with sexual sin.

My own failures as a high school and college student were driven in large measure by a narrow and simplistic view of how this battle works. One of the turning points in my struggle was listening to David Powlison give a talk on fighting sexual sin at a conference in 2004. He gave me a much fuller and clearer vision of the fight, which, when combined with the wise mentorship of my pastor, eventually led to patterns of purity and holiness that I didn't believe were possible.

For years I've incorporated Powlison's insights into my own counseling and teaching, using them to structure my own approach, even as I filled it out in various ways. A few years ago, that conference message was expanded into a book called *Making All Things New: Restoring Joy to the Sexually Broken*. It's a fantastic resource dealing with both sexual sin and sexual suffering, and addressed to both men and women. If you're looking for an additional resource for discussion and help, it's a good place to start.

In what follows, I'm going to loosely follow Powlison's structure and mention some of his insights, while filling out the picture and applying it in my own way. Here's his basic idea: faithfully and fruitfully fighting the war with sexual sin means we must recognize that it is a longer war, a wider war, a deeper war, and a subtler war.

Reactive Resolutions Versus Steady Resolve

Begin with the longer war. All of us wish we could simply snap our fingers and be free from sin. Sexual sin in particular fosters a kind of frustrated and discouraging impatience. When I was neck-deep in porn in my teenage years, I remember regularly making reactive resolutions about how I was going to change going forward. I would look at pornography, and then after wallowing in the guilt for a while, I would emerge from the pit and defiantly pronounce Job 31:1 over my life: "I have made a covenant with my eyes. How then could I look at a young woman?" The intensity of that declaration was matched only by the shame and discouragement I felt after eventually breaking that covenant.

I wasn't set up to fight for the long haul. I wanted a quick fix. I don't think I really recognized that sanctification was going to take the rest of my life and that it was going to be really hard. Nor did I realize that the longer war was by God's design. He's after endurance, and there are no shortcuts to endurance. Endurance *is* faithful-

All of us wish we could simply snap our fingers and be free from sin.

ness over a long period of time, in the face of seemingly overwhelming challenges. As a friend of mine puts it: "God wants men who can fight legions of orcs across the whole of Middle Earth, and the only way to get men like that is to actually have them fight legions of orcs across the whole of Middle Earth." But all of that was lost on my teenage self.

Since then I've become increasingly aware that progressive sanctification is a lifelong journey and a bumpy one at that. I'm always encouraged by the words of Isaiah 40:28–31.

> Do you not know?
> Have you not heard?
> The LORD is the everlasting God,
> the Creator of the whole earth.
> He never becomes faint or weary;
> there is no limit to his understanding.

> He gives strength to the faint
> and strengthens the powerless.
> Youths may become faint and weary,
> and young men stumble and fall,
> but those who trust in the LORD
> will renew their strength;
> they will soar on wings like eagles;
> they will run and not become weary;
> they will walk and not faint.

Young men grow faint and weary. We find ourselves exhausted and worn out by life and temptation. But Yahweh does not. He is the everlasting God, the Creator and Sustainer of all. And not only does he not grow faint and weary, but he *gives* power to us when we are faint and weary. In our weakness and discouragement, he pours into us his grace and might. In waiting on him, we find that our strength is renewed.

Notice the three "speeds" in the last verse. Sometimes we soar, flying like eagles through gracious skies. Holiness, love, and grace flow from us like water from a fountain. Sometimes we run, arms pumping as we make good time on the road to holiness. Sometimes we walk, faithfully plodding as we try not to envy our soaring and running brethren. And though the text doesn't mention it, sometimes we simply crawl in the right direction, straining inch by inch toward the heavenly city.

And that's the main thing: keep moving toward the new Jerusalem. Don't give up. Don't quit. Sanctification is a long journey, and our direction is more important than our pace. Let me say that again: *our direction is more important than our pace.* It doesn't matter how fast we're going; what fundamentally matters is that we're moving toward Jesus.

> Sanctification is a long journey, and our direction is more important than our pace.

Practically speaking, this means remembering that you can't get where you're going unless you start where you are. That means you have to be honest about where you are. Too often we want to spiritually bench-press 250 pounds when we're barely able to lift the bar. But setting impossible expectations for what you are able to do now is simply a recipe for frustration, discouragement, and despair. Instead we must begin where we are, not where we wish we were.

The Binge Trap and the Insidious Possessiveness of Shame

Now the previous paragraph might sound like I'm giving permission to sin. I'm not. Instead, I'm trying to be mindful of a particular kind of temptation. It's the tendency to reactively set unrealistic expectations and attempt to keep them by our own willpower, only to be crushed when we fail. We *never* have permission to sin. But rightly recognizing the reality of indwelling sin and the necessity of a long obedience in the same direction means we won't be sinfully wrecked by our failures.

Put another way, recognizing that it's a longer war with sexual sin is a way of avoiding the binge trap. This is one of the primary schemes of the devil in this area. First, he tempts us to sin sexually: to look at porn, to masturbate, etc. He draws us in with promises of orgasmic pleasure. Then, as soon as we give in, he turns on us and beats us with our failures. He goes from being the tempter to being the accuser. From seduction to condemnation. *You're a failure. You'll never get out of these chains. They own you.* This is both condemnation and a further temptation. It's another layer to the plot. When we've been walking in holiness for a time, Satan tempts us by allurement. Once we've failed, he tempts us through defeatism and shame. As we wallow in the guilt of the recent failure, we're more likely to sin again. We tell ourselves, *I've already blown it. I might as well blow it again.* So one failure turns into a pornography binge.

A counselor friend of mine refers to this as "the insidious possessiveness of shame." Often we don't even realize that we're stuck in powerful cycles of shame. We pursue pornography not only because of the fleeting pleasure of the sin but because acting out sexually subconsciously reinforces our shame-fueled identity, an identity that we don't even fully realize we have. This identity may flow from formative childhood experiences, from trauma and abuse, from broken and distorted relationships with parents, and countless other aspects of our lives. We may not consciously be aware of the way shame informs our patterns of behavior, but make no mistake, it frequently does. And shame is possessive. In its grip, we feel like sin owns us, like we are debtors to the flesh, like looking at porn is some sort of twisted obligation. And so we remain stuck in confusing and shameful cycles of bingeing.

I suspect that for some of you this is immensely relevant. Since you've started this book, you may have already looked at porn and masturbated. Your initial high hopes have given way to the reality that temptation is still very powerful, and you are still very weak. And so you must remember that this is a long war with many battles.

For some of you, the current battle is to avoid wallowing in your guilt and, instead, to cultivate new patterns of repentance. Without excusing your sin, you must learn to plow through failure. This means that when you fail miserably, you should repent thoroughly, seek forgiveness sincerely, make restitution quickly, make strategic adjustments wisely, and then move on. Don't get stuck.

And this is where a wise and godly mentor is so crucial. Their job is to bring hope and fortitude into the pit of guilt and shame. They are meant to be a model for where you are headed. It's important for you to see godliness on the ground and to believe that you can get there, knowing that someone cares deeply about you and is willing to walk a thousand miles with you on the journey of holiness. But even here, we must beware of a particular temptation. Your mentor's holiness could become an additional burden to you when you fail, tempting you to sink into the mire because of how far you have to go.

So remember, there is no virtue in wallowing in your shame and failure. Jesus died to break the cycle of wallowing. Paul says that ungodly guilt leads to despair and death, but repentance always leads to restoration and life. Even if you've failed in the past twenty-four hours, you still have a choice. You can either be the prodigal in the pig sty, eating the corn shucks and telling yourself, "I'm already eating it, so I might as well keep eating." Or you can get up and start walking back to your Father's house. Remember— it's never wrong to be the prodigal son coming home. Your Father is *always* ready and eager to receive you with a warm embrace, a magnificent robe, and a celebration you won't forget.

> It's never wrong to be the prodigal son coming home.

One final note. While acknowledging that this is a life-long battle should relieve a certain kind of false pressure and expectation, it can also be incredibly discouraging. Some of you might be thinking, *I can barely resist porn for a week. I don't have the willpower to resist for seventy*

years! And that's true. You don't. But God is not calling you
to resist for seventy years right this minute. He's calling
you to resist *today.* To resist *right now.* Faith and obedience
are always performed in the present, which is why God
gives us new mercies every morning, and exhorts us not
to be anxious about tomorrow, because tomorrow will be
anxious for itself. Sufficient for the day is its own trouble
(Matt. 6:34).

God doesn't give us grace in fifty-gallon drums we
can store in the basement. He draws us again and again
back to the fountain. He offers daily bread. In the words of
the old hymn, "I need Thee *every hour.*" So in recognizing
that we're in a longer war, don't lose sight of the present
moment, the present sacrifice, the present act of faith and
obedience. And most important, don't lose sight of God,
our loving and faithful Father, and our very present help in
time of need (Ps. 46:1).

A Word to Mentors

Compassionate Stability
and Focused Hostility

Continuing with the theme of gospel presence, we need to recognize that the first step in addressing deep-rooted sin is forthright and honest confession. You can't put to death a sin you won't confess. Hidden sins kill Christians because they are hidden. And your gospel presence as the pastor or mentor is designed to create an environment that invites your men to confess their sins, to be honest about their struggles, to overcome the natural aversion they have to exposing their shame. In other words, gospel presence aims to create an environment that is safe for sinners but not for sin. That's a key phrase: safe for sinners, not for sin. They are welcome; their sin is not. And there are two key aspects of gospel presence that matter for creating that environment. The first is what I call *compassionate stability*.

Compassionate stability means we aim to de-escalate the situation by leaning into the mess. Often men who are wrecked by sexual sin are filled with shame, fear of exposure, anxiety about future failure, and hopelessness about the possibility of change. They think, *If I admit out loud what I've done or seen or thought, then everyone will be so disgusted by me that they'll reject me.* Those kinds of emotions can overwhelm a man's desire to be honest about his struggle. And so the compassionate stability of gospel presence is meant to calm the broken, anxious, and weary sinner.

Compassionate stability leans into the mess. Your aim is to communicate that God is *for* them and *with* them through the fact that you yourself are *for* them and *with* them. This stability and calmness is not stoic; you should feel deeply for the men in your group. But your emotions are, by God's grace, under your control and direction so that you can willingly and compassionately lean into their sin. Broken sinners need to know that you're not recoiling in horror at them, no matter what they confess. They need to feel that you (and therefore God) are *with* them and passionately committed to their good.

Compassionate stability is especially important for properly naming the sins. Compassionate stability is what moves confession from "I've been struggling with lust" to "I've been having rape fantasies" or "I've looked at child pornography" or "I've started to be aroused by gay porn." Euphemisms keep us at the superficial level; men continue to be oppressed by guilt and shame because of the specifics of their lusts. When I've done sessions on fighting lust at our church, I regularly make a point of naming specific possible sins. I'll say something like, "You need to know that the pastors of this church are not afraid of your sin. We are for you because God is for you. And it does not matter how dark your darkness is. Whether it's rape fantasies or gay porn or bestiality or incest or child pornography, we are leaning in with the gospel of Jesus." Of course, I also make clear that there may be consequences for certain sins (child pornography is a big deal), but I want them to know that we will be with them no matter the consequences.[1]

This is one of the most important things that Bill, my pastor in college, did for me (though I didn't realize it at the time). When I would confess sin to him and find my mind racing and my nerves on edge and my emotions out of control with fear and shame, his presence and response to my confession always calmed me down. I may have been losing it, but nothing I said disturbed the deep and settled sense of peace and calm he had in Christ. He knew deep in his bones that God was bigger than my sin, that grace ran deeper than my brokenness. He lived and embodied by his presence the compassionate stability that I've since come to associate with Romans 8:31–39. This passage captures the spirit of compassionate stability as well as any in the Bible.

"If God is for us, who is against us" (v. 31)? God didn't spare his own Son but gave him up for us and will therefore freely and graciously give us everything (v. 32). No one can bring a charge against us because God himself has justified and approved of us (v. 33). No one can condemn us because Christ was crucified *for us* and raised *for us* and is now interceding *for us* (v. 34). Nothing can separate us

---

[1] If you are concerned that a confession might require more than personal accountability, please watch the videos at churchcares.com, specifically lessons 3 and 7.

from the love of Christ—not tribulation, or distress, or persecution, or famine, or nakedness, or danger, or sword (v. 35). God's all-conquering love means that every possible obstacle to our ultimate good makes us more than conquerors (v. 37). Death, life, angels, rulers, present things, future things, powers, height, depth, anything else in all creation—none of these can separate us from the love of God in Christ Jesus our Lord (vv. 38–39).

That's how committed God is to our good, and that's what Bill communicated to me whenever I would confess my sin to him. Our job as mentors is to internalize Romans 8:31–39 for ourselves and for those we lead. We must know in our bones that God is fundamentally *for us and with us.* And when we do, we are stable and compassionate, and compassionate stability makes an environment that is safe for sinners.

But there's another aspect to the right environment. Embracing broken sinners always entails a violent hostility toward their sin. If we're really committed to someone's good, then we will hate and resist those things that are harmful to them. And so it's necessary to combine compassionate stability with *focused hostility.* Focused hostility is still under control, but it includes a relentlessness and patience in exposing and killing sin. Without this focused hostility toward sin, we may find ourselves reluctant to challenge our men to pursue holiness. Our comforting may turn into coddling. But part of being a wise and faithful counselor to others means communicating the gravity of sin. The Bible minces no words about the consequences of making peace with ongoing sin: "If you live according to the flesh, you are going to die [eternally]" (Rom. 8:13). Those who practice the works of the flesh will not inherit the kingdom of God (Gal. 5:19–21; 1 Cor. 6:9–10). And the Bible uses intense and violent language to describe how we ought to resist sin: "Put [it] to death" (Col. 3:5–6; Rom. 8:13); "gouge it out" (Matt. 5:29); "cut it off" (Matt. 5:30); "flee sexual immorality!" (1 Cor. 6:18; 2 Tim. 2:22). These are words of violence and intensity that remind us that we can't make peace with our sin because the Holy Spirit will never make peace with our sin.

Gospel presence aims to communicate both that God is for you and your sin is not welcome. A man doesn't need to clean himself up to come to us or to God; he can come as he is. But we are committed to not letting him stay as he is. And so, with our demeanor and our words, we say, "I am for you; I'm leaning in; I'm not recoiling because of what you just confessed. I love you, and I'm with you, and I'm for you because God loves you and is with you and is for you. And I am so 'for you,' that I will never make peace with your sin. I will call you to put it to death, to cut it off, to run away."

Gospel presence says, "I love you; I'm for you; I'm with you. Now let's kill that sin."

6

The Wider War

One of the perennial temptations in fighting sexual sin is our tendency to isolate this struggle from the rest of our lives. It's easy to become myopic about sexual sin and pornography. One's spiritual life ends up revolving around the degree of success or failure or temptation in this one area. This struggle consumes all our attention and leaves other areas unaddressed. That's why it's important to widen the lens and to open up more fronts in the war.

Fixating on sexual sin in isolation from other sins and temptations will leave you stuck in cycles of failure. Often other sins are feeding lust, and failure to address them keeps us from fighting more strategically and wisely.

Sins That Steal Headlines and Sins That Fund Newspapers

Powlison describes this using a movie theater analogy. Sexual sin is a marquee sin. It gets all the attention. It's in flashing lights on a billboard outside the theater. But other movies are playing on other screens, and what happens on those other screens influences the strength of the sexual sin.

Another way of getting at the same idea is that some sins grab headlines and others fund newspapers. Pornography and masturbation are headline-grabbers; they cause intense amounts of guilt and shame and leave obvious devastation in their wake. Other sins, however, are more subtle. They're not on the front page, but they are secretly funding the paper. For whatever reason, most of us feel much greater guilt and shame over sexual sin in comparison to sins like pride, anger, envy, bitterness, and so forth.

The uniqueness of lust poses a particular danger for us. The devil piggybacks on it and hides other sins from us beneath the shame and guilt of sexual failure. As long as we are fixated on the headlines, we don't notice the sins that are funding the newspaper.

Powlison's chapter on this identifies some of the other sins that feed into sexual temptation. He tells the story of an unmarried man named Tom who throws a self-described temper tantrum in the form of pornography and mastur-bation on Friday nights, because his single friends are out on dates with their girlfriends and his married friends are home with their wives. In other words, sexual immorality may be grabbing the headlines in Tom's life, but entitlement, self-pity, and anger at God are actually what's funding the newspaper. And these sins are rooted in a more fundamental distortion, since Tom basically views his relationship with God in transactional terms. If Tom attempts to obey God, God should give him a wife. When God fails to keep his end of the bargain, Tom acts out. These subtler and hidden sins have given pornography a foothold in Tom's life.

If I were counseling Tom, I'd want to probe the roots of his entitlement and anger. Often anger is rooted in deep and unrecognized pain. Tom's sense of entitlement, anger, and self-pity are all connected to his view of God. I'd want to explore this further. Does Tom view God as a distant and unfeeling father? If so, why? Could that be connected to any significant situations in his past, perhaps his relationship with his own father or mother (more on this in chapter 8)?

Suffice it to say, Tom's struggles with pornography and masturbation are about more than simple lust and bodily release. Lust may be the presenting issue, but the real drivers are the other areas of sin—entitlement, anger, and self-pity. Powlison identifies other sins that often feed into lust and pornography use: envy, insecurity, approval-seeking, laziness, power hunger, and the like. Indulging in these sins is actually what gives sexual temptation so much of its power. That's why we must widen the war by opening up other fronts in order to make progress in walking by the Spirit.

Considering Our Weaknesses and Being Proactive

Widening the war also means that we recognize how lust and pornography exploit other weaknesses. It's harder to resist temptation when we're tired, anxious, depressed, or bored.

In one of his letters, C. S. Lewis listed four factors in his life that disposed him toward lust: sadness, disgruntlement, bodily weariness, and tea! These, he said, were the great dangers.

I once counseled a young man who was a late-night security guard at a parking garage. The job was boring, he was tired, and he had a smartphone with access to the Internet. And his exhaustion and boredom made sin easy and resistance hard.

The same is true of stress. For some men, pornography use is a way of coping with stress and pressure. Many men learn to cope with stress in this way in their formative years; they condition their bodies to deal with pressure by turning to pornography. And because of the body's plasticity, they retain this habit as they get older. When they feel stressed, they naturally gravitate to the sin as a way of relieving it. Thus, resisting sexual temptation must include

addressing the unhealthy and dangerous ways we deal
with pressure and stress and anxiety, as well as the other
hidden sins that contribute to sexual immorality.

Widening the battle is fundamentally about being proactive. Too many men treat sexual sin as if it is something
that just happens to them. Their mindset is almost totally
defensive: *How do I learn to resist the temptation when
it comes?* But as any good general will tell you, the best
defense is a good offense.

Powlison recommends that people who are stuck in
patterns of sexual sin begin to keep a journal in order to
help them recognize the wider issues at play. So, if you feel
stuck and don't know why, or if you're unsure of the wider
areas of the battle, you ought to begin to keep such a journal, recording the answers to basic questions like these:

1. Where and when were you tempted?
   What time of day was it?
2. How much sleep had you had recently?
   What about exercise? What had you
   eaten that day?
3. What pressures or anxieties had you
   been feeling in the days leading up to it?
4. How were your relationships? With
   your wife or girlfriend? With other
   men? With your kids or parents?
5. How are things at work? Any unusual
   pressures?

6. Any other sins and temptations come to the surface? Entitlement? Envy? Anger at God? Anger at your wife? Idleness? Laziness? Lowness?

7. How did you resist the temptation?

8. What kind of temptation was it? Be specific.

9. Does this sin feel familiar? If so, how far back does it go? Do you remember the first time you experienced it? Does it connect to any memories in your life?

10. What happened in the aftermath?

You don't have to write a dissertation—just enough information to be able to discuss it with other men in your life.

Keeping this sort of journal serves a number of additional purposes as well. For one, it provides its own kind of immunity to temptation by examining the nature and circumstances surrounding lust. C. S. Lewis noted that one of the quickest ways to disarm a lust is to turn your attention to the lust itself rather than to lust's object. Stop looking at the woman and examine yourself and your desires. Try to identify what lie you're currently believing. Because you can't lust and think about lust at the same time. Additionally, a journal like this will help you identify patterns of temptation and then take measures to anticipate and resist them. Lust will cease to be a mysterious force that just happens to you and, instead, become something that can be planned for and defeated.

Passivity, Idolatry, Blame

This sort of exercise will also expose how much we are sons of our father Adam. When the serpent tempted Eve, Adam was passive. The Bible says he was there during the temptation, but he said and did nothing until Eve gave him the fruit (Gen. 3:6). Then, having drifted in passivity along with his deceived wife, he takes up sin with a high hand. He listens to her and not to God. He chooses her over his Maker. Adam is not deceived about God's command; he heard it directly from God himself. Instead, he's idolatrous. And then, when he's exposed, Adam shifts the blame: "The woman you gave . . . me" (Gen. 3:12). He sins and then points the finger at God and his wife.

Passivity. Idolatry. Blame. Those are the hallmarks of Adamic masculinity, and it's a pattern that recurs through-out the Bible. When Moses is up on the mountain, the people come to Aaron demanding gods to worship. Aaron goes along with it, telling them to bring gold, which he then fashions into an idol. He leads them in false worship before the golden calf. When Moses comes down and interrupts the idolatry, Aaron, like Adam, blames the people: "You yourself know that the people are intent on evil" (Exod. 32:22). And then he acts as though the idol just happened: "They brought me the gold, I threw it into the fire, and out came the calf" (see v. 24). Same pattern: passivity, idolatry, blame.

When it comes to the fight against sexual sin, many men adopt a subtly passive attitude. It's often not fully conscious. It's a drifting. It's the rider allowing the elephant to steer. I think it's what Paul has in mind in Romans 13:14 when he exhorts us to "put on the Lord Jesus Christ, and make no provision for the flesh to gratify its desires." We are skilled at subtly making provision for the flesh. Long before we sin willfully and deliberately, we grease the skids. We'll ignore the patterns in our behavior. We'll resist attempts to widen the battle.

So let me echo the apostle: "Put on the Lord Jesus Christ, and make no provision for the flesh to gratify its desires." God has promised that he will not tempt you beyond your ability; he will provide a way of escape (1 Cor. 10:13). And he often provides the way of escape through proactive, strategic, gospel-driven planning.

If you know that Friday night is when you're prone to feelings of entitlement and self-pity, then you can't wait until you're alone on Friday night to start fighting. Because if you're honest, waiting that long to resist is generally a sign that you want to lose. Instead, God's way of escape is recognizing the breadth of your temptations and planning not to be alone that night. It's refusing to be led into temptation and giving room for the flesh to run wild. It's being proactive in putting to death the self-pity and anger at God before they flower into lust and masturbation.

Widening the battle is fundamentally about growing in self-knowledge. It's following the advice of the Puritan John Owen who exhorted his readers to learn their sin. Study how it works. Understand its tactics and strategies. Observe how the various sins and temptations intertwine and feed off of one another. And then make every effort to walk over the neck of your lusts. Walk by the Spirit, and you will not gratify the flesh and *any* of its desires.

A Word to Mentors

Probing the Present

At this point in your mentorship, you've hopefully established the right environment for your men, one that is safe for sinners but not for sin. You're practicing gospel presence, including both compassionate stability and focused hostility. As you're meeting, one of your goals should be to help your men interrogate their lusts. They need to become curious about the wider war, expanding "the front" so that it encompasses more issues in their lives.

For some, this will be uncomfortable. They may have joined the group to deal with "the lust issue." They may resist exploring wider patterns of sinful desires and behavior. So it will be important to stress how connected all of these issues are. Sins are rarely isolated. Widening the war is a matter of taking the fight with lust seriously. Refusing to explore the wider issues may reveal the "give me purity, but not yet" mindset. Be prepared to demonstrate the importance of widening the war.

This chapter offered an initial list of questions to consider as your men interrogate their lusts. Most of these questions focus on their present circumstances and temptations. In a future chapter we'll discuss the value of exploring one's past—formative childhood experiences, key events and relationships from the past, etc. In my experience, beginning with the present challenges is a good first step in cultivating an environment of honesty and trust.

Start with the list of questions provided and feel free to add to it. Offer it as a model for your men as they begin to grow in self-knowledge. Once they begin to understand their present patterns of temptation, they can begin to identify the lies they are believing and bring the gospel and the promises of God to bear on these patterns. If they are dealing with feelings of entitlement and envy, then perhaps it would be worth spending time exploring the grace of God: God does not owe us anything; he gives different gifts to people in his own time and way; he is wise in his distribution of grace and mercy; he is a good Father who knows how to give good gifts to his children, and he will never run out. Reflecting on and discussing these truths together from the Scriptures can help reshape the way your men are relating to God. So be prepared for your "lust group" to become much broader and wider. This widening is a sign of God's favor in bringing sin to light so that it can be confessed and killed.

7

The Deeper War

The deeper war is similar to the wider war, but whereas widening the battle focuses on drawing out other sins that feed into lust, deepening the battle is about untangling the knot of lust itself and seeing what hidden motives lurk within it. It's about pursuing sin into the hills and into the dark caves of the heart.

Of course, there's an important physical and bodily dimension to this struggle; men are drawn to the female body, and the physical sensations of sex are intensely pleasurable. But other dynamics are at work in our sexuality. For the present moment I'll focus on a deeply emotional component of porn use that often goes unrecognized. Sexual fantasies, whether on a screen or simply in the imagination, are about creating imaginary situations in which we see our strength and glory reflected in the desire and sexual satisfaction of a woman. I think this is a key dynamic for most, if not all, men who are dealing with pornography and sexual sin.

Two Key Facts

To understand this deeper aspect of this struggle, we need to understand a key fact about men and a key fact about sex. The fact about men is that we have a deep need to be admired and respected. Each of us wants to be a man among men. We want to be respected by those we respect. We want others to recognize and appreciate our abilities, strength, competence, and wisdom.

And not just other men. We want to be admired and desired by women, or at least, by one woman. We all want to be the man women want and other men want to be. And though this desire is inevitably corrupted in our fallen state, at root, it's divinely designed and good. Men should want to be strong, honorable, respectable, and admirable, and thus be honored, respected, and admired as men. That's the key fact about men.

The key fact about sex is that in sexual intimacy we receive pleasure by giving pleasure. By God's design the giving of pleasure to another is itself arousing and pleasurable. This is one of the beautiful gifts of the marital act—a husband and wife find that it's more blessed to give pleasure than merely to receive pleasure. We are hardwired to be aroused by the presence of another person's sexual pleasure.

Now both of these are facts of nature, and there is a connection between them. A man feels admired and validated as a man in the act of giving pleasure to a woman. He experiences his masculinity in a particularly potent way as he sees it reflected in the desire and pleasure of a woman. And this giving and receiving of pleasure finds its highest peak of satisfaction within the bounds of covenant love between husband and wife; it's a good gift from God in the context of marriage. And pornography is a particular corruption of this gift.

Mirrors for our Distorted Manhood

Pornography seeks to gain the pleasure of satisfying a woman without actually satisfying a woman. It's an attempt to get the pleasure and validation on the cheap—apart from the God-defined context of marriage. With porn you don't have to go through the hard work of being honorable, respectable, and admirable and winning a woman who will marry you. Instead, all you have to do is click. Or just play the fantasy in your imagination.

Thus, in pornography we are seeking mirrors for our distorted manhood. When a man views the video or images, or fantasizes in his own head, his eyes are on the woman, but what he's looking for is his own masculinity reflected in her imaginary sexual satisfaction. Her pleasure is a mirror by which he views his own strength, power, virility, and ability to satisfy. Her satisfaction is a validation of his masculinity (even though he's not actually satisfying her). In the fantasy her sexual pleasure is saying something to *him*. It's saying, "You're strong. You're powerful. You're desirable. I want you. I need you. You're a man." And that's arousing to men.

And, of course, this isn't limited to pornography and fantasizing. All sex outside of marriage attempts to gain the *feeling* of being a man without actually *being* a man.

This means that if a man is not admired or respected in his home by his wife, children, or—in the case of young men—parents, or if he is demeaned and belittled at work or at church, or if other men don't respect him, it's easy to turn to pornography for validation. The woman on the screen thinks he's amazing. If the masculine desire and need to be validated and admired as a man is not met in normal and healthy ways, then a man will turn to a corrupt surrogate.

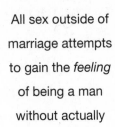

All sex outside of marriage attempts to gain the *feeling* of being a man without actually *being* a man.

As C. S. Lewis said, in the absence of food, a man will gobble poison. If respect and admiration are not found in the real world, then a man will content himself with a temporary fantasy.

The Imaginary Harem

None of this excuses pornography and masturbation. But it does help explain its pull and power. Lewis calls this aspect of pornography and masturbation the "imaginary harem."[1] Our sexual appetites, he says, are designed by God to take us out of ourselves, to send us into the world to find a spouse, and then to produce children (and grandchildren, and so forth). Sexuality, as I've said before, is meant to be fruitful. Pornography and masturbation, on the other hand, "send the man back into the prison of himself, there to keep a harem of imaginary brides."[2]

The longer a man lives in this prison, the harder it is for him to escape. A man in the grip of such lusts has enormous difficulty in pursuing and uniting with a real woman. The harem in his head (or on his computer) is "always accessible, always subservient, calls for no sacrifices or adjustments, and can be endowed with erotic and psychological attractions which no real woman can rival."[3] In the imaginary film that plays in his head or on the screen, "he is always adored, always the perfect lover."[4] In fact, the desire to be adored and admired as a "real man" is often as much a motive for pursuing the pornographic as any biological

---

[1] C. S. Lewis, "Letter to Keith Masson," *Collected Letters*, vol. 3 (New York: HarperOne, 2007), 758.

[2] Ibid.

[3] Ibid.

[4] Ibid.

or bodily appetite. But this fantasy makes no demands on his selfishness; "no mortification [is] ever imposed on his vanity."[5] The imaginary harem, in the end, simply becomes "the medium through which a man increasingly adores himself."[6]

In my experience, it's important to highlight this dimension of the struggle for sexual holiness. A man in the grip of lust is searching for more than just the release of a bodily appetite. He's often looking for validation. We must recognize the emotional need that is fueling our lust and then ask: Where is that need meant to be satisfied?

> A man in the grip of lust is searching for more than just the release of a bodily appetite. He's often looking for validation.

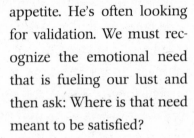

Sin is always a corruption and perversion of a good impulse and desire, and one of the chief aims of the kind of honest and guided conversation with godly men that I'm advocating is to cut through the corruption and perversion, identifying the good desire underneath the sin. Once that desire is identified, we can channel it in fruitful and God-honoring ways. We want to recognize the real good we are seeking and then kill the parasite that has twisted it.

---

[5] Lewis, "Letter to Keith Mason," 758.
[6] Ibid.

Identifying the Good Beneath Our Desire for Validation

In the present case I think there are layers to the real good in question. The most basic and fundamental level is divine approval. Our deep need to be validated is ultimately met in God's glad-hearted approval of us in Christ. God is happy with us. The gospel is good news because it offers to us unbridled divine love, acceptance, approval, and yes, even admiration. The promise of one day hearing, "Well done, good and faithful servant" (Matt. 25:23) is a potent weapon in the fight against lust. It signals God's fundamental orientation toward us. We might say, in a manner of speaking, God is proud of us in Christ. Or, to use the biblical language, he is "not ashamed to be called [our] God" (Heb. 11:16). That's the fundamental validation we need.

Building on this foundation, we seek to have God's fundamental validation echoed in the validation of our community. As Lewis says in a letter, "Love of every sort is a guard against lust."[7] For a married man, this begins with his wife. Her respect and admiration really matter to him. Her sexual desire for him matters to him. A wife who truly respects and desires her husband, and who communicates that respect and desire in tangible ways, is giving her husband powerful weapons in his fight for holiness. The same is true of other women in his community, whose respect

---

[7] Lewis, "Letter to Mr. Pitman," *Collected Letters*, 919.

he desires in the way a boy desires the respect and admiration of a sister. Lewis notes in one place that ordinary female society—engaging appropriately with women as image bearers of God and sisters in Christ—helps promote our own chastity. To return to a point I made in an earlier chapter, spending appropriate time among women keeps a man from seeing women as objects of sexual consumption.

Beyond the respect of women, a man looks to other men to affirm that he is one of them. He wants to be a man among men. At work, at church, and in the world, a man is looking to be affirmed and appreciated for his gifts, abilities, and accomplishments. He wants to receive the respect of those he respects. Of course, respect is something that can't be flippantly given. Tell a man, "No, really, I respect you," and he will feel pitied and patronized. Thus, there's a bit of a "chicken and egg" problem in fostering a community of mutual respect. Respect should be earned, and thus a man must *act* respectable in order to *be* respected. He must *do* something admirable in order to be admired. At the same time, showing a man respect is often an effective way to induce him to act honorably.

The best course is for each of us to attend to ourselves first. Drawing on the fact of God's approval of us in Christ, we ought to seek to be respectable, godly, and admirable men—regardless of whether anyone else notices. At the same time, we ought to love our neighbors by being alert to admirable traits in them and then signaling our recognition. And here the indirect approach is often as important as the direct one. Don't just say to a man, "I think you're wise." Ask him his advice. Don't just say, "I think you're honorable." Give him a position of honor. Or better, give him responsibility. For men know that's the true validation for our masculinity.

Masculinity (like femininity) is something that emerges through a shared mission or endeavor. When the fact of our maleness meets the reality of the challenges we face together, masculine virtues rise to the surface. Strength, wisdom, and competence in their varied forms show themselves, and the "band of brothers" phenomenon comes into play. Mutual respect among godly men who expect holiness and exhort one another to it is a protection against all manner of temptations. That's one of the reasons I'm writing this book to a group of men: I want to create an environment where you can look each other in the eye and say, "We're going to kill our sin and become the men God wants us to be."

Now I know that all of this talk of being admired and respected is dangerous. It might easily become a form of self-worship and people-pleasing. But I'm simply trying to express something Paul repeatedly gives voice to in the pastoral epistles. He encourages Christians to live godly and dignified lives that please God (1 Tim. 2:1–4). Elders, as the leaders and exemplary men in the congregation, should be sober minded, self-controlled, and respectable (3:2). They must "have a good reputation among outsiders" (3:7). Deacons, too, must be dignified and tested (3:12). Paul echoes this in his letter to Titus, where he exhorts older men to be "self-controlled, worthy of respect, sensible, and sound in faith, in love, and endurance" (Titus 2:2).

These are traits we ought to aspire to, and we should want them to be recognized and validated by others. What keeps this from being self-worship is the recognition that all of these are gifts from God. They are reflections of his worth and character. They are achieved with his strength and help, as he works in us what is pleasing in his sight. Though we are active in our pursuit of holiness, sanctification is ultimately the work of God. Thus, all human boasting is nullified, and all glory is given to God. For what do we have that we did not receive? (1 Cor. 4:7).

A Word to Mentors

The Emotional Dimension

In my experience, the emotional component of the struggle with pornography is often overlooked. As we've seen in the last few chapters, lust is complex and interwoven with other needs, desires, and sins. For many men, pornography use is a way of coping with other frustrations and struggles in life; it's a temporary escape from the grind of life. This doesn't excuse the sin; God still hates and forbids it. But it does help the sin become in some sense understandable.

At this stage in the fight, a chief part of your goal is to help the men in your group learn to interrupt their lusts and look behind the curtain to see what's animating their desires. What lies are they believing about God and about themselves? What frustration or anger or anxiety is producing the discontentment that makes pornography seem so attractive?

I knew of a situation where a young father was frustrated with where he was in life. He wasn't in the job he wanted; things were hard at home; he envied the success and blessing of other men his age. All of these produced a deep frustration and discontentment in his life, and he turned to pornography as an outlet. My counsel to him was to recognize that he didn't mainly have a lust problem; he had a discontentment and envy problem. In working with him and his wife, my goal was to help him to recognize when discontentment, envy, and covetousness would arise in his heart. Long before the temptation to lust came into view, these other sins were wearing down his defenses. He was believing lies about himself—*I'm worthless and stuck in my job; God will never use me for his kingdom; I'll never measure up to the fruitfulness of my friends; it's never going to get better.* And he was believing lies about God—*God doesn't love me; he doesn't want to bless me with valuable labor; he's indifferent to my struggles in life.*

These were the lies he had to learn to recognize early so that he could preach truth to himself. This was also a way to engage his wife more in his own struggles, since she could relate more to his struggle with discontentment and encourage him to be a faithful husband and father. She began to express her gratitude to him for providing for their family, even if he wasn't in his preferred job. They talked more about what God wanted to do for and with their family for the kingdom, which gave him a sense of purpose and something worth fighting for.

My point is this: when you reach this stage in helping men fight, there's no telling where things might go, what deeper issues might surface. But God is faithful and ready to help his people pursue holiness in all areas of our lives.

8

Sexual Brokenness

Before turning to the subtleties of the war, I want to take a moment and change the lens. As I said in the introduction, I tend to default to warfare imagery. We are engaged in a fight, a struggle, a war with sexual temptations and desires. I've been greatly helped by David Powlison, who introduced me to the paradigm of a longer, wider, deeper, and subtler *war*. I've also made use of the addiction lens, especially when considering sexual sin's effect on the body (see chapter 4).

Reflecting on the wider and the deeper war is a great opportunity to explore the third lens—the lens of sexual brokenness. I've been especially helped in this regard by a book called *Unwanted* by Jay Stringer. While Stringer and I would emphasize slightly different approaches to overcoming unwanted sexual desires (he's less keen on the language of warfare and violence), his work on understanding the deeper motivations and wounds beneath sexually destructive behavior is excellent. In fact, you can consider this chapter a review and recommendation for Stringer's book.

Listen to Our Lusts

Stringer's book is the fruit of his own counseling practice and extensive research on unwanted sexual behavior. (Thirty-eight hundred people participated in an in-depth survey that informs many of his conclusions.) He targets a broad range of sexually broken and destructive behaviors, from pornography to hookups to prostitution. He addresses the sexual brokenness of both men and women. His primary call is that we must learn to "listen to our lusts."

Sexual brokenness, he says, is revelatory. The specifics of our sexual struggles are not random, but are often tied to our formative experiences, especially in childhood. Only by considering the particular shape of our sexual brokenness will we discover the deeper wounds, needs, and factors that are at play in our sexuality. As he says, "Whereas scars reveal external wounds, unwanted sexual behavior often reveals internal ones."[1] Stringer encourages us to be curious about our sexual behavior, to engage our sexual

---

[1] Jay Stringer, *Unwanted: How Sexual Brokenness Reveals Our Way to Healing* (Colorado Springs: NavPress, 2018), 57.

stories, to view them as road maps to the deep places of our souls.

Stringer argues that our present sexual brokenness results from the convergence of two rivers: our formative experiences (especially in childhood) and our present challenges. He notes that sexual arousal is not static; it typically constructs a story, with a setting and a plot, and by paying attention to the plot, we can uncover how our formative years influenced and shaped our "arousal cocktail"—the constellation of images, fantasies, objects, and situations that sexually arouse us.

For example, he identifies the ways dysfunctional family systems leave deep wounds on the soul. Whether rigid families that shame members into compliance with strict rules or disengaged families that foster a felt need for belonging and affection, these types of dysfunction form us in ways that negatively affect our sexuality. We pursue pornography and sexually destructive relationships in order to fill the void created by the hypocrisy or abandonment we experienced in our upbringing.

Abandonment, in particular, often creates a calloused hopelessness and felt sense of worthlessness. As a result, adults who were shaped by parental abandonment pursue sexual behaviors that reinforce that sense of worthlessness. According to Stringer, people with such stories are not merely in pursuit of pleasure; they are also driven by the self-contempt that their broken sexuality confirms. As we noted earlier, shame is insidiously possessive.

He also discusses the effects of childhood triangulation, a form of "emotional incest" in which a child is called upon to meet the emotional needs of one parent. This produces a somewhat predictable array of marital challenges (triangulated people struggle to "leave and cleave") and sexual dysfunction (emotional incest can become sexualized, leading people to pursue incestuous pornography). And, of course, childhood trauma—whether cataclysmic or long-term—and sexual abuse leave deep wounds that often manifest in our sexuality. The humiliation and violence children endure can play out in destructive sexual behavior as adults.

Significantly, Stringer notes that there's a difference in the way trauma and abuse frequently affect men and women. Men tend to attempt to overthrow the power dynamics of their childhood by imagining or inflicting sexual harm on others, whereas women tend to repeat the humiliation in their own sexual humiliation and degradation. Women repeat and reenact the harm done to them (one thinks of the millions of women who were captivated by the sadomasochism of *Fifty Shades of Grey*). Sexual abuse victims often feel overwhelmed by a kind of "sexual madness" characterized by intense shame, especially if their bodies were in any way aroused during their abuse. To them, the arousal indicates a complicity in the abuse, which leads to intense feelings of disgust and self-contempt. As adults, abuse victims will often return to the sexual blueprint of their abuse, reenacting the ugly mix of secrecy, shame, and pleasure in their own behavior. The bottom line is that a significant aspect of resisting sexual sin in the present is healing the sexualized wounds we incurred as children.

When it comes to our present experiences, Stringer highlights a number of destructive patterns that fuel unwanted sexual behavior. In this, his analysis dovetails with Powlison's "wider war." For example, he identifies relational deprivation and dissociation as key factors influencing broken sexuality. When we deprive ourselves of meaningful relationships and cease caring for our basic needs (such as healthy diet, exercise, recreation), we easily fall into patterns of dissociation which involve escaping from people and responsibilities. We numb ourselves with Netflix, video games, and social media, and these distractions pull us away from the hard work of relationship building and, thus, become gateway drugs for sexual sin. This type of dissociation is often a cover for a sense of futility and meaninglessness in life. When we lack purpose, we default to pornography and other sexually broken behaviors for short-term pleasure and distraction; the shame-filled after-effect then reinforces our felt worthlessness.

> When we lack purpose, we default to pornography and other sexually broken behaviors for short-term pleasure and distraction.

Anger and Lust

One of Stringer's most insightful observations involves the connection between anger and lust. He notes that Jesus treats these two passions together in the Sermon on the Mount and does so in similar ways. Underneath murder is anger. Underneath adultery is lust. The biblical commands reach far beyond the level of action; they confront us at the deeper level of the heart.

Lust and anger fuse together in many forms of sexual sin, whether it's pornography, strip clubs, or prostitution. In fact, Stringer provocatively claims, "I have never met someone who struggles deeply with lust who is not also battling with unaddressed anger."[2] Sexualized anger is often rooted in that sense of futility and powerlessness in life. Stringer quotes one man who said, "With porn, I am served. In real life, it's as if I am the one on my knees, subservient to what everyone is requiring of me."[3] For men like this, a chief dimension of the arousal is the prospect of ordering a beautiful woman to serve them. Their lust is an eroticized anger and hunger for revenge; the degradation of beauty is part of the corrupt desire itself. The more the anger goes unaddressed, the more corrupt and perverse the sexual appetite becomes, and the more shame and secrecy surround it.

[2] Stringer, *Unwanted*, 103.
[3] Ibid., 43.

There's much more in Stringer's book, including examples of the connections between the formative experiences and the present behaviors, as well as extended counsel on pursuing a path of healing and transformation that integrates the self, relationships, and community. My summary here is merely meant to point you to a few other angles on the wider and deeper aspects of the war and to encourage you and the men around you to be curious about the patterns of your sexual desire. With the help of a wise counselor, probe the specifics of your sexual fantasies. Question the deeper motivations beneath the surface of porn addiction. The specifics are revealing, and true victory and healing will only be possible as these deep desires, pains, and needs are brought to light and addressed by the gospel.

A Word to Mentors

Unearthing Deep Pain

In past chapters, we've discussed the importance of widening the war by probing the present struggle. This chapter highlights the role the past plays in shaping our present patterns of temptation and sin. A central goal of deepening the war is to connect past formative experiences to the present patterns of temptation. This requires asking additional questions that will unearth some of these formative experiences and relationships. Here is a sampling to get you started:

1. Does this struggle with sin feel familiar? How far back does it go in your life? Do you remember the first time you experienced this?

2. Does this struggle with sin (whether lust or the wider issues) connect with any particular memories (even if they don't have an obvious connection)?

3. Describe, as best you can without being overly graphic, your "arousal cocktail." Are you drawn to particular kinds of fantasies or pornography?

4. Does the connection between anger, frustration, and lust resonate? Given that anger typically arises from some felt injustice or pain, does anything come to mind in your past?

In addition, you may want to begin to ask questions about key formative relationships—with father, mother, and siblings. Whether it's a distant father or a possessive mother, a bully of an older brother or a boundary-crossing sister, these relationships have an immense impact on the way we're shaped and can illuminate some of the hidden drivers of our struggle with sexual sin. Again, Stringer's book may be helpful to you as a mentor in providing categories and possibilities for exploring the connections between the present and the past.

Two more comments on exploring the deeper dimensions of the struggle. First, probing the past may be an exercise best done in a more one-on-one setting rather than in the group. Use wisdom in discerning whether it's best to press into the depths as a group of men, or whether exploring the past might best be done in a more private setting.

Second, if you begin to explore the way past experiences intersect with present struggles, don't be surprised if you unearth deep pain. Some of your men may begin to unravel in surprising ways. This is not a sign of something going wrong; it may be the beginning of a deeper work of grace that will bring healing and restoration. However, you will want to be prepared in case things begin to unravel for some of your men. Be ready to direct them to wise pastors and Christian counselors if you feel you're over your head in what you've unearthed. Humility means knowing the limits of your wisdom and being able to rely on the wisdom of others who have had experience with abuse, childhood trauma, and deeply broken family relationships.

At the same time, don't underestimate the power of your own gospel presence. You may not have answers for all of the challenges brought to light, but you know the living God. You have his Spirit. And your role in this story may be to cling to the hope of the gospel and communicate compassionate stability to your men, even as you direct them to wise guides who can better address the deep pain and brokenness of their lives. In my experience, the most fruitful and restorative counseling situations I've been involved in have included a layered and interwoven approach to pastoral care. Pastors, lay leaders, small groups, and wise Christian counselors were involved. Each of us brought different things to the situations. But we all worked together to be the body of Christ for hurting and broken members. And God was faithful.

9

The Subtler War

The last step in expanding our view of the battle explores the subtleties of the war. This involves learning to distinguish different types and degrees of sexual sin and to respond accordingly.

Unfortunately, when it comes to how they respond to their failures, many men unwittingly treat having an orgasm as an arbitrary line in the sand. A Christian who looks at pornography and has an orgasm feels intense guilt and shame in the aftermath. However, if he stops short of an orgasm, he feels some measure of victory, even if he looked at pornographic images for half an hour. He feels he can fantasize, imaginatively indulging his lust, so long as he stops short of actually reaching sexual climax. He sometimes even feels this if the reason he failed to have an orgasm is owing to some circumstance outside of his control—as in, he heard his roommate come in the front door so he closed his browser and stopped indulging. It's possible for a man in that position to rejoice that God "provided the way of escape," when, in fact, he was swimming in sexual sin for the previous hour. The reality is that repentance is still necessary, whether one has an orgasm or not. By indulging himself, he has stoked the fires of lust and made it harder to resist the next time.

Picture the soul as a city surrounded by walls. The conscience is the watchman on the walls. Now if an army of orcs appears on the horizon, conscience will raise the alarm, and the whole city will move into action. But if, instead, sin sneaks into the city two by two, we tend to ease up. We don't diligently address the small temptations and compromises. And then one day we wake up, and the city is burning because we've let in dozens and dozens of enemies over the last week, always in tiny increments.

Augustine said that we should not despise "light" sins, since many light objects make a great mass. Every river is made from a vast number of small drops. Compromise has a compounding effect, which means we can measure our progress in holiness by the sensitivity and alertness of the conscience. A dull conscience swims in filth and doesn't recognize it. It acclimates to worldliness and immorality. It breathes in poison that numbs and deadens the spiritual reflexes. And then, when the opportunity for the big sin comes, it buckles. Thus, it's crucial to avoid making masturbation and orgasm the be-all and end-all of this fight.

There are biological reasons orgasm becomes the line in the sand. It's when the pornographic upper shifts to the pornographic downer through the opiate release, and with the sexual thrill in the past, we become immediately susceptible to the guilt, condemnation, and shame that follow failure. But part of wisely learning to resist temptation means repenting of lust in all of its forms and not just when it leads us over the cliff of orgasm. In fact, that's another good image for how many men fight. Picture a hill with a steep cliff at the bottom. Having an orgasm equals getting knocked off the cliff. Now imagine a large boulder at the top of the hill. What many men try to do is to get as close as they can to the cliff's edge without going over. They plant their feet at the bottom of the hill and then watch as the boulder rolls down toward them. They foolishly think they'll be able to stop the boulder at the bottom of the hill, after it's built up a good head of steam. And so they find themselves inexplicably bowled over the edge again and again. Instead, your goal should be to fight the battle as high up on that hill as possible.

Different Levels of Lust

Powlison uses a video game analogy to describe the varying levels of lust.[1] The idea is that the earlier levels of a video game are easier than the later levels. As you progress

---

[1] In principle, this analogy could be applied to any sin.

in the game, the enemies get harder and the skills needed to win become more complex. He likens that to the different levels of the fight with lust.

The first level is what he calls "high effort, high cost" sins. These are things like adultery and going to a strip club. They require a lot of effort; you have to actually find another person to participate. When they are finally exposed, they are often the most devastating. Because of their visibility, when people are delivered from them, there is much rejoicing.

The next level includes "lower effort, lower cost" sins. This is the level of Internet pornography. We don't have to find another person; we simply have to click a link. Nevertheless, there is still a level of intentionality involved and certainly a cost associated with repenting or "getting caught."

After this, there are the "no effort" sins. This is what happens late at night when you're lying in bed and sexual images flash through your imagination. Perhaps you recall images you've seen in the past. You don't need the computer; the images and fantasies are at your mental fingertips. Obviously, such sins are harder and more difficult to fight since they often appear without warning, or when we are particularly vulnerable (such as when we're tired or stressed).

A step beyond these sins is the "sins that come looking for you." Assume a man is not committing adultery or indulging in Internet pornography. What's more, assume he is faithful to push unwanted images out of his mind when they intrude. He still has to face the lingerie billboards in Target, or the provocative images on the magazines at the checkout counter, or the scantily clad young woman jogging when the weather warms up. He doesn't go looking for these images; they come looking for him.

Finally, Powlison highlights what he calls "atmospheric sins." These have to do with the ruts in our mind that we've cut over the years. When we see a woman, where do our eyes immediately go? Do they check her out and size her up? Regardless of what she's wearing, do our eyes and imagination begin to flow in a lustful direction? This is the highest and most difficult level to fight because it has to do with our immediate instincts and intuitions.

I highlight Powlison's video game analogy to make one basic point: where you choose to fight is where the battle will be fought. If you draw the line at masturbation and orgasm, then the battle will take place at that point, and you will likely win some and lose some. But the goal should be to press forward so that we are fighting as close to the atmospheric level as possible. We want to be resisting at the level of double takes, channeling our instinctive responses in a godly and healthy direction. Rather than letting the boulder get rolling down the hill, we want to stop it at the top, as soon as it begins to move. We want inertia to be our friend, not our enemy. You may still lose some battles near the top. Your eyes may still wander, and your thoughts may flit in ungodly directions. But losing battles at the top is a different affair from losing at the bottom.

This is also one place where we must wisely set our expectations. As soon as you resolve to fight the good fight earlier, as soon as you begin to trudge up the hill to keep the boulder at the top, the battle will get more difficult. You should expect it to get harder. You should expect your body—which, remember, has been habituated to sin—to lash out and fight back and steer toward the lusts in order to get the dopamine hit. You should expect the principalities and powers to alter their tactics and look for an opening. None of this should be surprising to you.

Sometimes we think if we sincerely attempt to obey God, life will get easier. But in fact, the opposite is often the case. I'm reminded of a line from *The Horse and His Boy*: "Shasta had not yet learned that if you do one good deed your reward usually is to be set to do another and harder and better one."[2] The reward for completing a task is to be given another, harder task. This is how God grows us up into maturity. Thus, the increased difficulty as we set ourselves to climb the hill is a good sign. We're no longer a lowly private; we've been promoted to captain. Getting clear on this is vital for plowing through failure on the way up. Expecting difficulty means that when we get knocked

---

[2] C. S. Lewis, *The Horse and His Boy* (New York: HarperCollins, 2002), 146.

down, we get back up again. We repent, we learn, we adapt, we fight better.

Changing the Channel

A significant part of fighting early is learning to rein in the imagination. The imagination is a part of the lower faculties, part of the elephant. You might think of it as the gateway to the soul. It's a key interface between the bodily senses and our intellect and will.

Picture the imagination as a screen in the mind. The world, the flesh, and the devil can throw things up on the screen. An image or a sound or a scenario can flash across it. We can't always control what gets thrown on the screen. But we can control what stays there. The choice before us is whether to let the tape play or to change the channel.

I stress *changing* the channel because it's hard to fight something with nothing. You have to replace one image with another because there will be *something* on the screen. Attempting to look at a blank screen won't work; the tempting images will simply reappear. We must find something else to think about.

My own view is that we should use any weapon at hand. One pastor I know will imagine Christ on the cross—beaten, bloody, crown of thorns on his head—in order to drive away lust. Jonathan Edwards, the eighteenth-century pastor, would pose complex mathematical and theological problems to himself in order to resist his sinful appetites.

For my own part, I have a number of different "channels" I turn to when faced with temptation. One of them I call "the aftermath." I imagine the conversation with my wife after I've sinned. I imagine the look of pain and disappointment and hurt on her face. I never want to see that look again. I imagine my boys finding out and being confused by what their dad has done. I think about the implications for my ministry, since self-control and discipline are prerequisites for being a pastor. I love pastoring and teaching, and the prospect of disqualifying myself through indulging in lust often breaks through the seductive lure.

Beyond the aftermath, I'll consider the promises of God and his goodness toward me. I'll remind myself that God has approved and accepted me, that he is well-pleased with me. I count my blessings (literally), reminding myself of all of the good—both earthly and spiritual—that he has done for me. And then I use his past goodness as a reservoir to launch me forward to his promises of future joy and pleasure at his right hand. I wield the things of earth in the fight for holiness. Deeply enjoying God in and through all of his gifts immunizes me to the false and seductive pleasures of sin. It's one reason I wrote my book *The Things of Earth*; I know from experience that deep enjoyment of legitimate earthly pleasures exposes the shallowness and bankruptcy of the worldly corruptions. What's more, I don't want to lose my enjoyment of such innocent pleasures. I know that indulging in sin brings a heaviness that hangs on the soul and taints joy in sunsets and baseball and barbecue.

Finally, if these other means don't work, I'll engage in holy distraction. I might drop and do push-ups. I might get up and clean the house. I'll find anything I can to distract myself from the images.

I recall one time the temptation was unusually intense. The typical means to "change the channel" were ineffective. The images and fantasies kept coming back, no matter how many promises I remembered or how much I considered the aftermath. My eventual solution was to pick up a sci-fi novel. I knew my imagination would quickly become engrossed in the story, and the elephant would calm back down. And it worked. I lost myself in the book until my eyes grew heavy and I drifted off to sleep.

The fundamental thing is to pray earnestly for God's help and *not give up*. I'm always reminded of the words of Hebrews 12:4, "You have not yet resisted to the point of shedding your blood." What a picture. "I've been resisting the temptation, Lord, but it keeps coming back." "Yes, but are you bleeding?" In other words, if the image returns, push it away. If it comes back, push it away again. How many times should you change the channel? As many times as it takes.

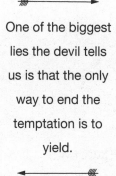

One of the biggest lies the devil tells us is that the only way to end the temptation is to yield.

One of the biggest lies the devil tells us is that the only
way to end the temptation is to yield. We must retrain ourselves so that we know from experience that the temptations are not permanent; they will diminish.

Good Pretending

It's important to stress that the imagination isn't simply
the devil's playground; it can also be a great help in the fight
with sin. One of the ways it does so is by helping us to be
true "doers of the word." That phrase comes from James 1.
Here's the full passage.

> But be doers of the word and not hearers
> only, deceiving yourselves. Because if any-
> one is a hearer of the word and not a doer,
> he is like someone looking at his own face
> in a mirror. For he looks at himself, goes
> away, and immediately forgets what kind
> of person he was. But the one who looks
> intently into the perfect law of freedom and
> perseveres in it, and is not a forgetful hearer
> but a doer who works—this person will be
> blessed in what he does. (vv. 22–25)

James contrasts doing the word with being a mere
hearer. Hearing without doing is like looking at your face
in a mirror and then walking away and forgetting what you
look like. So "hearing" = "looking in the mirror," and "not

doing" = "walking away and forgetting." Simply *hearing* the word is not the same as *obeying* the word. If all you do is hear, without doing, you're kidding yourself. There must be something more than hearing.

What's the "more"? It's looking in the right mirror and *doing* what you *see*. So what's the mirror? The mirror is the law of liberty, what James earlier calls "the word of truth" by which we're born again (James 1:18), the "implanted word" which is able to save our souls (James 1:21), and which later he calls "the royal law" of liberty (James 2:8, 12). In other words, the mirror we should look carefully into is the Holy Scriptures, both Old and New Testaments, understood in light of the good news of King Jesus. That's the Word we are to do. In other words, we're after *gospel* doing. Now what does that mean?

The gospel doer looks into the mirror of the royal law of liberty. The gospel doer sees himself reflected in the living and abiding Word of God. Doing the Word, or what I'm calling "gospel doing," means you look to Jesus and to yourself in Jesus for the strength and supply for all of your deeds. You have been raised with Christ. You are seated with him in the heavenlies. Your life is hidden with Christ in God. One day, when he appears, you also will appear with him in glory (Col. 3:1–4). Your true self, the fullness of who and what God made you to be, will be revealed and made manifest. But, for now, it's hidden.

Gospel doing means you see yourself in God's royal law and then *live into that vision*. You look into the mirror, and you don't walk away and forget. You persevere in that vision. You do what you see. This is more than just moralism or even moral exemplarism. It's not simply, "What would Jesus do?" I find that question often too abstract and distant to be of much use. Instead it's, "What would I do, if I were full of Jesus?"

C. S. Lewis called this "good pretending." Bad pretending is hypocrisy. It's when we pretend to be something we're not. Our pretense, our fakery, is a substitute for reality. Good pretending is when the pretense *leads up to* the reality. It's what children do when they pretend to be grown up so that they can grow up. And it's what Christians do, in our pilgrim condition, when we're told to do the Word.

Practically speaking, it works like this: imagine what you'd be like if you really did experience deep, gospel renewal—if you really believed that the living God was for you and that he would meet all your needs. Imagine that version of yourself, the one that is free and happy and stable and full of love. Now take that imaginary you and put him in the situations you face in your life. If you really did love God deeply from the heart, and if you really did love your neighbor sincerely, what would you do? When you have the answer, ask for God's help and then go and do it (even if you suspect that your motives are mixed).

In other words, do the deeds of love even when (some of) the substance is lacking. Don't wait for your motives to be fully pure. Repent of your impure motives, your sinful preferences, your spiritual apathy. Look at yourself in the mirror of the gospel, the liberating law of King Jesus. See what you are in light of the good news. Now don't walk away and forget. Remember. Persevere in that vision of yourself in Christ. Walk away and do what you saw, even if you don't fully feel what you saw. And, James says, you will be blessed in your doing.

This has relevance for the pursuit of holiness in general, but also to the fight with sexual sin in particular. For starters, this is one way to change the channel of the imagination. When tempted to lust, imagine what you would do if you were godly, stable, and full of Jesus. What would the "gospel you" do? That kind of question defuses the lust by moving the focus from lust's object to our own response. And it recovers the imagination by deploying it in the pursuit of holiness.

Incidentally, this is one reason godly mentors are so crucial in recovering the imagination. A godly mentor provides a life worth imitating, a concrete example that strengthens the imagination of others so that obedience, fidelity, and stability become real to them. Men come to see the outline of their own future faithfulness and self-control in the mentor's present faithfulness and self-control. They grow in their ability to imagine what it looks like for *them* to walk by the Spirit because they see their mentor presently walking by the Spirit.

Even more than that, James's exhortation dovetails nicely with the picture of grace-driven sanctification in Romans 6. In chapter 4, I mentioned the two primary

exhortations Paul makes in that passage, one concerning
the mind and one concerning the body. However, it's worth
a more detailed look to see the fuller picture.

In this section of his letter, Paul is attempting to show
that the gospel of God's grace and the justification of the
ungodly do not lead us to continue in our wickedness.
Though grace abounds when sin increases (Rom. 5:20–21),
we shouldn't sin *so that* grace abounds (Rom. 6:1). Those
who have died to sin cannot still live in it (Rom. 6:2). We
have been baptized into Christ and therefore baptized into
his death (Rom. 6:3). The whole purpose of this union—
signified and represented in our baptismal burial—is that
we would be raised to "walk in newness of life" (Rom. 6:4).
Union with Christ in his death will necessarily lead to
union with Christ in his resurrection life (Rom. 6:5). The
old man—Adamic humanity that is habituated to sin and
subject to the curse—was crucified with him; as a result, we
are no longer slaves to sin (Rom. 6:6). Christ, having been
raised from the dead, now has complete dominion over
death (Rom. 6:9). He died to sin, once for all, and he now
lives to God alone (Rom. 6:10). Christ, as the head of the
new human race, is free from the penalty, power, and presence of sin and death.

Based on the acts of God in Christ, and based on our
union with him by grace through faith, Paul gives this
exhortation: "So, you too [note how the exhortation flows
from the preceding verses] consider yourselves dead to
sin and alive to God in Christ Jesus" (Rom. 6:11). Here is

the mental act, the imaginative act that we're called to do. We are to "consider ourselves," to "imagine ourselves," as it were, in a particular way—dead to sin and alive to God. Now this imagining is no mere fantasy; it's rooted in the reality of what God has done, just as gospel doing begins with seeing ourselves in the mirror of the law of liberty.

Following the mental and imaginative act, we come to the bodily dimension—we refuse to let sin reign in our bodies. We no longer obey our passions (Rom. 6:12). We are no longer governed by the unruly elephant. Instead of presenting our bodily members to sin as instruments for unrighteousness, we present ourselves to God as new, resurrected men, and we present our members to him as tools of righteousness (Rom. 6:13). We no longer offer our members to our old slave master for his purposes. Instead, we offer ourselves to a new Master, and we wield our bodies for his righteous purposes. The grace of God has set us free from sin's dominion and the hard tutelage of the law (Rom. 6:14) so that we can now be conformed to the image of Jesus.

In the end, we have only two options. Either we present ourselves as slaves to sin, or we present ourselves as slaves to obedience (Rom. 6:16). One pathway leads to increasing lawlessness, impurity, shame, and, in the end, to death. The other pathway leads to increasing righteousness, sanctification, and, in the end, to eternal life (Rom. 6:19–23).

In both James and Paul, then, we begin with Christ's work and God's revelation. In light of what Jesus has done, we see and consider ourselves in a particular way. We see ourselves in the mirror of God's Word. We consider ourselves in light of Christ's work. And then, building from

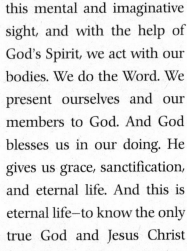

Either we present ourselves as slaves to sin, or we present ourselves as slaves to obedience.

this mental and imaginative sight, and with the help of God's Spirit, we act with our bodies. We do the Word. We present ourselves and our members to God. And God blesses us in our doing. He gives us grace, sanctification, and eternal life. And this is eternal life—to know the only true God and Jesus Christ

whom he sent. In his presence is fullness of joy, and at his right hand are pleasures forevermore (Ps. 16:11).

A Word to Mentors

Imagination and Dreams

As men begin to make progress in resisting sexual temptation, they may begin to experience nocturnal emissions ("wet dreams"). These can be especially frustrating because they are often accompanied by highly sexual dreams. It's important to help shepherd your men in how to think through this aspect of the struggle. A few truths are worth keeping in mind.

First, the shift from actively seeking pornography and masturbating to being afflicted by a sexual dream is significant. It should be first seen as a sign of growth and success in fighting sin. The devil is resorting to attacking your imagination while you sleep. In most cases, this is because other avenues of temptation have been closed off. So take this as a sign of progress in holiness.

Second, consider the presence of wet dreams as more of an affliction than an action. It's something that happens to you, not something you do. We have limited control over what images are thrown onto the screen in our minds when we are awake. How much more when we are asleep? Regarding sexual dreams as an affliction is important because it places expectations in the right place. Sins must be killed; afflictions must be endured.

Third, faithfulness with your waking imagination can, over time, lead to less sexualized dreams. Think of it this way: past pornography use has supplied a reservoir of corrupt images and scenarios in your memory. The devil makes use of those in manipulating your dreams. As you walk in faithfulness, the power of those images in your memory will diminish. There will be less of a foothold in your memory for the devil to exploit. A shift in the dreams may take a long time (as in years). But long-term faithfulness will frequently have a positive effect on the quality of the dreams.

Fourth, should a wet dream happen, a wise approach is to de-escalate the situation. Don't try to recall the dream. Don't wallow in the feelings of guilt that may accompany the dream. Resist them with the gospel. Commit your way to the Lord. Ask for his grace and protection from the terrors of the night (which includes the devil who seeks to destroy us when we're at our weakest). Move past the dream and, as much as you can, try to forget it.

10

A Word to Young Men— Single, Dating, and Engaged

By now you should have a decent idea of the landscape of the battlefield as well as the nature of the war. It's longer than we often expect. It's wider than we often recognize. It's deeper than we sometimes realize. And when we begin to fight, it becomes subtler than we could've foreseen.

In the last few chapters, I want to offer some particular wisdom for men at different stages of life. The contours of the battle shift as a man changes stations in life from singleness, to dating and engagement, to marriage and children. It's good to recognize how these principles of the fight apply in these different stages.

Restoring Control of You to You

I want to begin with young men, as young as middle school and through college. The fundamental challenge of young adulthood is learning to tame the passions.

When puberty hits, the hormones go coursing through the body, and the elephant takes on a mind of his own. Taming the unruly elephant is the central task for young men. Of course, the Bible commends self-control to all of us. Elders are to be self-controlled (1 Tim. 3:2; Titus 1:8). Older men are to be self-controlled (Titus 2:2). Older women are to be teaching young women to be self-controlled (Titus 2:5). In these cases, Paul's exhortation to self-control is embedded in a list of other virtues.

But when it comes to Paul's exhortation to young men, there's only one thing on the list: "Encourage the young men to be self-controlled" (Titus 2:6). This is the chief challenge for young men, especially for the unmarried. In fact, if a single man is unable to exercise self-control, Paul urges him to marry so he doesn't burn with passion (1 Cor. 7:9).

If you're a young man reading this book, then the fundamental thing you need to learn is self-control. You must learn to control yourself, to master yourself, to rule yourself. And as a Christian, you must do so in reliance on the grace of God in the gospel. Self-control is a fruit of the Spirit (Gal. 5:22–23). When the Spirit begins to work in your life, God will restore control of you *to you*.

Of course, ultimately, God does the work. The grace of God trains us to renounce ungodliness and worldly passions and to live self-controlled, upright, and godly lives "in the present age" (Titus 2:11–12). Notice that. *Grace* trains us. God does the work.

But when God works, he doesn't work in a vacuum. He doesn't work *apart from our efforts*, but *through our efforts*. The passions are not tamed apart from our will but are brought to heel by our sanctified will. God doesn't simply zap us into holiness. Instead, he works in our lives so that we master our thoughts, our eyes, our hands, our imagination. We take our thoughts captive. We bring them in obedience to Jesus (2 Cor. 10:5). We present our members to him as instruments of righteousness (Rom. 6:13).

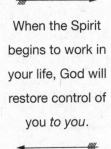

When the Spirit begins to work in your life, God will restore control of you *to you*.

This is both our work and God's work. We work out our salvation because God is at work in us "to will and to work according to his good purpose" (Phil. 2:12–13). The Spirit of God reorients our rider so that, with our minds set on Christ, we learn to direct and regulate the unruly elephant.

Practically speaking, what do the words *self-control* and *self-mastery* mean? Controlling self means *I* tell my eyes where to look. *I* tell my mind what to think about.

I control what plays on the screen of my imagination. *I* am in control of my members because I'm walking by the Spirit, and he is graciously restoring control of me to me.

Winning Small Battles

I find this particularly helpful when it comes to dealing with "the sins that come looking for you"—things like double takes or the magazine rack or the billboard along the highway. These sorts of temptations aren't just opportunities for sin; they are opportunities to recognize God's work in my life in cultivating self-control. In seasons when I've felt the pull of sexual temptation more strongly than others, I've sometimes anticipated and even welcomed small temptations like this in order to get a clear and decisive victory in the battle. Driving down the street, I know there's a billboard ahead that poses a temptation. I anticipate the struggle, commit it to the Lord, ask him to grant me mastery of my impulses and members, and then I keep my eyes straight ahead. (I tell my eyes where to look; they don't tell me where to look.) And after the battle is won, I thank God for his work in my life. My eyes are not my masters. God is restoring control of me to me. This keeps me from getting stuck in the mire of temptation and adopting a defeatist attitude about the fight. Victory, like defeat, is contagious.

And self-control isn't only relevant to lust. In fact, a young man who only seeks to be self-controlled with his sexual appetites will likely find them to be stubborn and powerful. Self-control spreads. This is where the wider war becomes relevant. God's call to young men is to develop a Spirit-wrought self-mastery over all of the passions—lust, anxiety, anger, depression, envy, discontentment. The common thread in each of these cases is that they are immediate and impulsive responses to external events and circumstances. Provocative images come up on the computer screen, and the elephant steers toward them. The big test or the big game or the big dance looms on Friday, and the elephant rears in anxiety. Parents exert control on our lives, or friends turn their back on us, and anger rises in our hearts. A girl rejects our romantic advances, and sadness and depression kick in. Or a friend gets a girlfriend, or a great job opportunity, or has success in life, and envy and discontentment immediately grab us by the throat.

In each of these cases, what's needed is Spirit-wrought mastery of the passions. I've known situations where the presenting issue is pornography and masturbation, but the true issue is discontentment, depression, and envy. Wrestling those impulses to the ground and learning to fight them with the promises of God is crucial. Mastery of envy and lowness will carry over in the efforts to master the sexual appetites.

Or again, consider what James tells us about taming the tongue. "The tongue is a fire" (James 3:6) that sets the world ablaze. Humans have tamed all kinds of beasts and birds, "but no one can tame the tongue" (James 3:7–8). But he also says, "If anyone does not stumble in what he says, he is mature, able also to control the whole body" (James 3:2). In other words, taming the tongue is unbelievably difficult, basically impossible for humans on their own. A thought comes into the head and makes a beeline for the mouth. The man who, with God's help, is able to bridle the tongue and bring it to heel, who is able to govern his impulsive speech, will also be able to bridle the rest of the body, including his sexual impulses and urges. Self-control spreads.

Accountability and Faithful Fathers

There are two other words of wisdom for young men in particular (though they're really relevant for all). The first has to do with accountability groups.

My experience of peer-level accountability in high school was abysmal. The groups were basically big puddles of sin, where young men who were getting mowed down by lust would commiserate with one another. The fact that none of us were able to make significant strides in holiness over extended periods of time had a subtle yet profoundly discouraging effect on all of us. Rather than spurring one another on to love and good deeds (Heb. 10:24), our meetings together made us wonder whether victory was even possible.

That's why it's especially important for young men to be mentored and accountable to godly men who have seen significant victory in this area and who are models of God's sanctifying holiness, who have won battles and carry the aroma of Christ. Young men need to know that holiness, however imperfect, is possible. Sexual sin doesn't have to be a stronghold in their lives. What's more, compromised men rarely call others to take greater responsibility for their actions or wisely provide strategic counsel. There may be a kind of fellowship when you meet a fellow wallower, but neither of you will be of much use in getting out of the pit.

The corollary of the call for better accountability for young men is the need for faithful fathers, whether biological fathers or fathers in the faith. Too many dads have disqualified themselves from helping their sons. Their present failures render them largely useless in equipping their sons to resist temptation. I know that this may be a sensitive subject for some readers. Some fathers may feel the greater weight of shame because of the generational effects of sin (whether potential or actual). At the same time, fatherly affection and the desire to spare our sons the devastation and wreckage of sexual addiction can be a powerful motivation in our own fight. The sexual threat to our kids is real. Ease, accessibility, the potency of the polydrug—all of these loom as our kids grow up in a technological and pornographic world.

When I think about my own boys reaching puberty and facing this challenge, I want to be able to say, "I know it's hard, but it's possible to resist. It's possible to steer the elephant. It's possible, by the grace of God, to be a man of integrity." And I want to be able to say that *because I've lived it*. I don't want them to get there and be forced to say, "You just have to learn to live with the failure." I believe we can do better for our sons and daughters.

When You're Dating or Engaged

Everything I've said thus far in the chapter applies equally to men who are single and men who are dating or engaged. But dating and engagement also raise the stakes for the fight. There's now another human being intimately involved, so the devastation caused by lust is far more extensive.

At the same time, a godly man now has something more concrete to fight for. He wants to be the sort of man who is worthy of this woman's attention and trust. In other words, while the counsel is the same, the man who is dating or engaged has an added motivation. A single guy may want to grow in holiness so that he's ready to lead a wife, but his future wife is an abstraction. A man who is dating or engaged has the motivation in front of him; she's real and concrete.

So if you're dating or engaged, then my first exhortation to you is simple: beware of simply transferring lustful attention from the computer screen to your girlfriend or fiancée. A young man who has been enslaved to pornography, who has weaponized his body so that sin is easy, may find that the new woman in his life inspires him to resist temptation more vigorously. He wants to kill the dragon in his own heart so that he can get the girl. But it's also possible for her to become the temptation. If he begins to starve the beast of the food it's used to, it may simply turn to new food. Sin finds a new outlet. This is especially true once a couple becomes engaged. The commitment level is high. The emotional intimacy is increasing. And yet the sexual intimacy must still wait. But the rising emotional intimacy and the fact that the wedding day is in sight means it's much easier to rationalize pushing boundaries with each other. A simple kiss and an affectionate hug begin to give way to making out and heavy petting. And like with pornography use, where you choose to fight is where the battle will be fought. Many couples can track the battle line as it steadily moves closer and closer to fornication, and yet they feel a certain powerlessness in the face of it.

Often the boundary pushing is rationalized because a young man wants to communicate to his fiancée that he finds her beautiful and desirable. And so the couple begins to engage in foreplay while still attempting to stop short of intercourse. But that is exceptionally difficult because that's where making out and caressing are *designed* to go. They are gifts from God that are meant to lead to the marital act. The couple who engages in foreplay is attempting to board the train of sexual intimacy and then jump off before they get to the end of the line. They get the boulder rolling down the hill, but still want to stop it at the bottom before it carries them over the cliff.

That's one reason that, in general, I discourage couples from long engagements. Paul says it is better to marry than to burn with passion. Extended engagement is basically like trying to stand near a bonfire for one year, two years, three years. The longer the engagement, the greater the temptation, the more likely the sin, the deeper and more lasting the consequences. So the second exhortation is: get married; don't just burn with passion until it consumes you.

No matter how long or short the engagement, the temptation is still real. The passions are still easily aroused. Given the way a couple's desire for each other mutually feeds and strengthens such passions, the goal is to find some deeper reasons to resist that pull that can counterbalance its strength. If sexual gravity is pulling them into the black hole of immorality, we need to employ powerful rockets in order to escape.

In my experience in premarital counseling, one of the fundamental ways I try to provide that boost is by reframing their resistance to sinning sexually with each other. Because we ultimately want emotional intimacy, spiritual intimacy, and sexual intimacy to be united together in marriage, it's difficult to suppress one type of intimacy (the physical) while the others are growing and increasing. The pull to sin with each other is strengthened by the good and right desire they have to know each other, to pursue each other, to be one with each other. But engagement is precisely the season of life in which emotional and spiritual intimacy are growing, while sexual intimacy is waiting. So in this difficult season my goal is to provide additional incentive to resist the pull of sexual temptation with each other. In the counseling session I'll tell them both (and especially the man) something like this: "The fundamental thing you're doing in engagement is demonstrating to your future wife that you're trustworthy. In order to fully and rightly give herself to you in marriage, she needs to trust you. She needs to know you can be confronted by a beautiful woman, who is attracted to you and desires you and wants to be with you, and you can resist that temptation. She needs to know you can meet the forbidden woman and walk away. In marriage, you don't know who the forbidden woman will be. But in engagement, you do. You're engaged to her. From the perspective of your future wife, your fiancée *is* the other woman."

The Opportunity of Temptation

In other words, I want the couple, and especially the man, to see the opportunity engagement provides. He has the chance to show his fiancée that he can say no both to porn and to her. His integrity and self-control are vital in winning and keeping her trust so that the marriage is healthy and holy. And while she won't be there at midnight when he's tempted to look at porn on his computer, she is there at 9:00 p.m., when they're about to watch a movie alone together and considering whether to cuddle on the couch. And whether she knows it or not, she's learning about his self-mastery by how he relates to her. "Here is a woman who is not your wife but who loves you, desires you, and wants to be with you. Can you resist? Can you honor your God? Can you remain faithful to your wife?" That's the question facing an engaged couple.

In other words, if you're dating or engaged, I want to reframe the temptation you face with your significant other. I want to harness your noble desire to be faithful to your future wife against your present desire to commit sexual immorality with your fiancée. I want you to say yes to your wife by saying no to your fiancée.[1]

This really is crucial for engaged couples. It is a beautiful thing when a wife can give herself freely and unreservedly to her husband. When I think about it, I'm often reminded of something C. S. Lewis wrote about his marriage to his wife, Joy: "For those few years [Joy] and I feasted on love, every mode of it—solemn and merry, romantic and realistic, sometimes as dramatic as a thunderstorm, sometimes as comfortable and unemphatic as putting on your soft slippers. No cranny of heart or body remained unsatisfied."[2]

---

[1] To be clear, I'm not suggesting that your fiancée is (necessarily) trying to tempt you; I'm simply recognizing the mutual temptation your relationship provides and calling you to take the initiative in guarding your marriage. Your goal should be to practice and prepare to be her head by resisting your improper desire for her now.

[2] C. S. Lewis, *A Grief Observed* (New York: HarperOne, 2001).

That kind of freedom in marriage is profound and deeply satisfying. But that kind of freedom only comes from deep trust.

The inverse is true as well. A couple who sins together in engagement will carry the consequences into marriage. There will be a taint, a kind of stain on their intimacy. Their sexuality will often be colored by the guilt and shame that lingers from their sin during engagement. Trust was broken then, and the brokenness persists. They've each seen firsthand that, in the right circumstances, sexual desire can overpower the godly will of their spouse, and that knowledge, even when it is unrecognized or subconscious, has a distorting effect on the marriage.

So if you're engaged, remember this: no Christian married couple ever wishes that they were more physical in engagement. No godly couple ever looks back and says, "I wish we were less prudish during our engagement. I wish we had pushed more boundaries together." Instead, the most common thing you'll hear from many is, "Why couldn't we have waited? Why couldn't we have held off? Wouldn't our early months of marriage together have been sweeter if

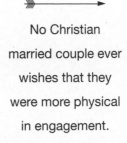

No Christian married couple ever wishes that they were more physical in engagement.

we had laid a foundation of trust, stability, and godliness

with each other?" That's the opportunity that dating and engagement provides. The motivation to be holy is more real, the consequences of failure are more dire, and the reward of walking by the Spirit and refusing to gratify the desires of the flesh is more satisfying in a healthy and holy marriage.

A Word to Mentors

Confessing to a Fiancée

"Should I confess my sexual sin to my girlfriend?" This is a common question from unmarried men who are struggling with pornography. As a general rule, I don't think a man should confess such sins to his girlfriend. It's placing a burden on her that she does not need to bear. She is not his wife. He is not her husband. He has not violated a covenant with her, and she is not in a position to offer help and aid to him in the struggle. If he's going to confess to others, it ought to be to godly men who are able to understand the struggle and help hold him accountable. Thus, I discourage Christian men from confessing their pornography use to their girlfriends.

Things, however, change when a couple is engaged to be married. Part of premarital counseling should involve discussion of sex, and this discussion ought to include some discussion of one's past sexual sin (and current struggles). This is an area that is particularly tense and fraught, and wise pastors and mentors are particularly important in facilitating and debriefing such conversations. A mentor and his wife can offer invaluable help and stability as a couple works through the challenges of past and present sexual sin.

At the same time, a man should be careful not to make his fiancée into his accountability partner. As we discussed in chapter 2, healthy habits of confession involve confessing to God first for fundamental forgiveness, confessing to godly men for healing and counsel, and then, if necessary, confessing to one's wife for restoration. A man's fiancée occupies an "in-between" position, one that's more significant than a girlfriend but not a wife. As a mentor, your role will be to help engaged couples navigate what healthy habits of confession look like in this unique season of life. As you do so, you should ask two fundamental questions:

1. What will help each of these people love God and grow in holiness?
2. What will help each of these people determine whether they ought to get married to each other?

11

A Word to Married Men— The Watchdog and the Caged Animal

In this chapter I want to address some of the complications that arise in marriage as a result of sexual immorality and how these complications actually prolong the struggle and patterns of failure rather than reduce them. At this point, I'm assuming some measure of progress in implementing the strategies we've discussed. Creating space, starving the beast, patterns of confession and accountability, fighting the battle in its various dimensions—all of that is already ongoing. Assuming that a man has begun to emerge from lustful habits and patterns, what sorts of additional challenges should he expect, particularly if he's married?

Let's frame it this way: I've already noted that the devil has schemes, plots, and plans. That notion comes especially from 2 Corinthians 2:11, where Paul urges the church to "not be taken advantage of by Satan. For we are not ignorant of his schemes." Recall what we know of that situation in Corinth. A man had sinned egregiously (we don't know the details), and, in doing so, he had caused great pain to the church. The church had punished him, and he is apparently repentant. However, it seems the church is somewhat reluctant to welcome him back. They don't want to forgive him and comfort him. Paul writes, urging them to reaffirm their love for him because that's what obedience to God requires. And then he makes the comment about outwitting the devil by knowing his schemes.

In other words, there are layers to the devil's plots in a situation like this. The first layer is to get the guy to sin gravely. Having succeeded there, the plot thickens. Now the scheme is to get the guy to hide it. That fails and the sin is exposed. Now maybe Satan wants the church to tolerate the sin (like the Corinthians do with sexual immorality in 1 Corinthians 5), to refuse to exercise church discipline. But assuming the church administers discipline, the plots aren't over. Now the goal is to get the church to refuse to accept the sinner when he turns back. In other words, neither success nor failure removes Satan's schemes. There's always a counterattack ahead.

It's like the television show 24. You remember how each season went? There's an assassination plot against the president. By episode 6, Jack Bauer and the team are closing in on the culprit. But you know that this show is called *24*; there are 18 more episodes. And so you know there's going to be a twist. The plot will thicken. And sure enough, it does. The assassination attempt on the president is a cover to get the nuclear codes. In episode 12, when they capture the bad guy with the nuclear codes, it's revealed that this was a smaller part of a plan to acquire biological weapons, which are now in the hands of the bad guy's boss. And on and on it goes. That's how the devil operates. There are layers of plots and schemes. There are contingencies for when you succeed and when you fail. When you fail, the plots involve wallowing, bingeing, and crushing guilt. When you succeed, the new plots involve pride, self-reliance, and coasting. But the important thing for us is that there's always a deeper plot. And we must be aware of it.

A Devilish Plot: The Watchdog and the Caged Animal

Now, when it comes to marriage and the fight with sexual sin, I have a particular plot in mind. It can emerge when a husband is still in the grip of pornography, and it can persist long after he's become porn-free. I call it "the watchdog and the caged animal," and it has to do with the cycles of reaction and overreaction that a husband and wife fall into in seeking to fight sexual sin and recover from sexual failure.

The basic idea is that a husband's sexual sin fosters fear in his wife. It often activates her insecurity, and out of that insecurity she seeks to take action to protect herself. So she becomes hypervigilant, identifying sexual temptation wherever they go. In other words, she becomes a watchdog.

Her hypervigilance, in turn, reinforces to him that he's a caged animal, always on the brink of indulging sexual passions. One whiff of sexual temptation, and he could fall over the cliff. Thus, her fear fosters anxiety and hypervigilance in him. Now, when he goes out in public, he's on edge. He wants to guard his eyes, and so he's constantly on the lookout for billboards, images, and attractive women, all of whom are threats. He becomes unable to have normal interactions with women at work or at church, viewing them as inherently threatening.

Meanwhile, his wife picks up on his hypervigilance, and her fears that he's on a sexual hair-trigger are reinforced. And so, when he begins to squirm when an attractive woman walks by, or if she notices him noticing the pretty waitress, or perhaps sees his eyes linger too long in a particular direction, she's deeply hurt, as her worst fears are confirmed. His failure feeds her fear. Her fear feeds his sensitivity. His sensitivity becomes a jittery anxiety, and this anxiety reinforces her fear, with the result that even a simple date night becomes filled with land mines. The mere presence of an attractive woman or a provocative image makes the whole thing blow up. And the conversations in the aftermath do not help. He's unable to explain the nature of the temptation. She's unable to understand why he can't have eyes for her only. And they become unable to enjoy a night out together.

Now this type of couple thinks they have a sexual sin problem. But they don't. They have an anxiety and reactivity problem. That's the deeper plot. That's the dynamic that is fueling the sexual temptation. That's what's funding the newspaper, while the attractive waitress steals all the headlines. And to the degree the couple continues to move in cycles of hypervigilance and reactivity, they will remain stuck and frustrated, and the wall between them will get bigger and bigger. What's more, the likelihood of serious sexual sin will ironically get higher and higher.

It's possible for a couple to adjust in some measure to this type of dynamic. With his wife watching him like a hawk, he orders his food while staring steadfastly at the menu (and only at the menu). He learns to live with the sensitivity on his Attractiveness Radar turned up to eleven. She learns to live with the regular pain caused by his double takes and his anxiety in the presence of attractive women. She may even come to appreciate his curtness and rudeness to attractive women. The problem is that these dynamics are never static. They will spread. Because he won't just be short and rude to the waitress. Instead, there will be conversations like this:.

"Why are you always rude to my friends?"

"I'm not rude to your friends."

"Yes, you are. You don't smile at them.
    You won't talk to them. You look angry
    whenever they walk up."

"No, I don't."

"Yes, you do."

"Well, if I do, it's because I don't want you
    to think I find them attractive. I want
    you to know that I only have eyes for
    you."

"Do you find them attractive?"

"*What?* No! I mean, I don't know. I mean,
    they're nice. Some of them are pretty.
    And that's why I might be a little stand-
    offish to them. I don't want them or you
    to get the wrong idea."

"But I want you to be kind to them. They're
    my friends, and they think you don't
    like them."

"I don't like them. I mean, I don't like them
    in that way."

"Just try to be nicer, okay?"

"I will, but . . . I don't know how, exactly. It's
    complicated."

"I just don't get you."

The watchdog and the caged animal create a dynamic
where any woman not related to a man by blood or

covenant is a live threat to his holiness and his marriage. And he treats other women that way—from the waitress to his wife's best friend.

A church culture where this dynamic has taken root is profoundly frustrating for everyone involved. Women feel that they are constantly viewed as temptresses, regardless of their modesty and holiness. Men project anxiety and instability in social settings, as they try to "flee sexual immorality" (1 Cor. 6:18) by fleeing the presence of women. They're constantly telling themselves, "Don't think about sex," and therefore they constantly think about sex. What begins in a right desire for sexual purity and propriety ends in cycles of misunderstanding, overreaction, and frustration.

The wife-as-watchdog doesn't change the fundamental distortions of manhood and womanhood. Men are still regarded as beasts who can't control their appetites. Women are still sexualized as objects. The difference is that the beasts are now fixated on avoiding the objects at all costs, always mindful of the watchdog's fearful and angry gaze. This is a common scheme of the devil, and growing in wisdom means learning to undo the reactive dynamic at play.

Making Distinctions: Temptation and Sin

Undoing this dynamic begins with acknowledging two things: (1) the desire for holiness and purity is a good thing; (2) the cycle of reactivity and mutually feeding spousal sins is not. Our goal is to keep the pursuit of holiness while breaking the cycle of reactivity and hypervigilance.

But how? In my experience, it takes a lot of honest and guided conversation between husbands and wives. I say "honest" because the reality is that many couples simply can't talk about the struggle honestly. The pain is too deep; the sin is too fresh. Communication breaks down. And that's where the "guided" piece comes in. Many couples will need help from outside the marriage in order to have the hard conversations and untangle the destructive patterns at play. That's one reason I've written this book for men who struggle *and* for men who want to help. I'm hoping that mentors and their wives will be able to foster these sorts of conversations and calm the reactive emotions that so easily get out of control.

The first thing worth noting is that fidelity helps. The conversations are difficult because the wounds are fresh. However, as a man demonstrates seriousness and stability in his pursuit of holiness, as he applies the sorts of strategies we've discussed in earlier chapters, he will (hopefully) find that the conversations with his wife become easier. They won't be as fraught and tense because he's not constantly reopening the wound.

What else is involved in untangling these dynamics? We have to learn to make key distinctions. The first is between temptation and sin. One of the key schemes of the devil is to flatten this distinction. Satan took Jesus up on the mountain, pointed to all the kingdoms of the earth in their glory, and said, "Look." And Jesus did not sin simply because he saw the kingdoms of the earth. It wasn't a sin for him to see them. It was a sin to receive them as a gift from the devil. In other words, it's the act of the will that assents to the temptation that constitutes the sin. The temptation itself is not damnable. Jesus was tempted yet without sin (see Matt. 4:1–11).

Now, of course, there are important differences between Christ's experience of temptation and ours. While in his humanity it was possible for him to be externally tempted to sin, his mind and body were not inclined or habituated to sin as ours are. In other words, whereas temptation often finds a ready home in our hearts, Christ's holiness and perfection mean that, while he was truly tempted, the temptation didn't grab him in the way that it grabs us. He is the perfect resister of temptation. In fact, he resisted to the point of shedding his own blood. As C. S. Lewis said, a man who succumbs to temptation knows how strong it is up to that point.[1] But Christ knows the full

> Awareness of beauty is not sin. What you do with that awareness might be.

---

[1] C. S. Lewis, *Mere Christianity* (New York: HarperOne, 2015), 142.

strength of temptation since he is the only One to resist it completely. Nevertheless, the example of Christ gives us this important distinction. Noticing the attractive waitress at the restaurant isn't a sin. What one does with that "noticing" could be. Awareness of beauty is not sin. What you do with that awareness might be.

Clarifying Our Language

But even once the distinction is made, husbands and wives can still miss each other because of the different ways we experience temptation and because we may use different language to describe it. For example, early in our marriage, my wife and I got stuck over the use of the language of "attraction." The discussion centered around whether there is a difference between finding someone *attractive* and *being attracted to* them. For me, these were synonyms: if someone is attractive, it means that I am, at some level, attracted to her. For my wife, these were different. *Attractive* is an adjective; it's a quality of a person that says something objective *about them*. On the other hand, "being attracted" to them says something *about me*. It implies a movement toward them on my part. This category confusion caused a lot of frustration between us.

"Are you attracted to her?"

"Sure."

"And you're okay with that? How can you say that?"

"Wait. You're attracted to other men some-
    times, right?"

"No, never!"

"You mean to tell me that you never find
    other men attractive or handsome?"

"Of course I do."

"Okay, now I'm seriously confused."

In other words, if I said I was attracted to someone, my wife heard, "I'm leaning in. I'm giving in. I'm allowing myself to be drawn to her. I'm assenting to something sinful." In my mind, this language confusion was rooted in a common difference in the way men and women experience temptation. In general (though not always), men are highly visual. That is, finding someone attractive (and therefore being drawn to them in some way) is triggered simply by seeing them.

Women, on the other hand, in general have a much more emotional and relational component to attraction. While they recognize when a man is handsome or attractive, it doesn't have the same initial impact. In order for them to "be attracted to" him, there must be something more than the visual, usually some kind of emotional or relational connection. And this emotional or relational connection often takes time to develop, whereas the visual orientation of the man is much more immediate.

In fact, this is another place where the tiered psychology I sketched in chapter 3 can be useful. All people, whether men or women, have an instinctive or intuitive awareness of beauty and attractiveness. However, for men, this awareness is highly visual and more sensitive than in women. The sense apprehension and sense appetite (those are the lower faculties) detect "woman as beautiful" all in one instant. A man can see a woman out of the corner of his eye and immediately form an impression about her attractiveness. Now, he may not always be right. He may look more closely and discover that she isn't as attractive to him as his initial impression suggested. My point is simply that the forming of the impression is automatic and immediate. A man sees a woman at a distance and has an instinctive reaction ("She's likely attractive.") or at the very least, an instinctive curiosity ("Is she pretty?").

Now this phenomenon produces deep anxiety and fear in conscientious men who are trying to walk by the Spirit. They're anxious because the conclusion ("she's attractive") is reached with no chance for rebuttal or interruption. Beauty is simply seen, attraction is intuitively acknowledged, curiosity is immediately aroused. The elephant forms a judgment before the rider has a chance to do anything.

When this recognition of beauty is identified with sinful lust, then the only possibility of victory is total avoidance. And total avoidance requires hypervigilance, which feeds and strengthens the watchdog and caged animal dynamic. What's worse, in these circumstances the immediacy of the sense impression leads a man to feel like a constant failure. He's defeated before he's begun. He despairs of change and is in serious danger of bingeing because he thinks, *Resistance is futile, so why bother fighting?*

Learning to De-escalate

My point in walking through this is twofold. First, it's simply to note that the differences in our experience as men and women often lead to different definitions of terms, which, in turn, lead to much confusion and frustration, especially when the relationship is tense because of past sexual failure.

Second, progress comes when we learn to de-escalate the situation by making the proper distinctions. Recognizing the beauty and attractiveness of the opposite sex is natural. There's nothing inherently wrong with it. Women are beautiful. And they don't stop being beautiful because a man gets married. A godly man ought to be able to acknowledge such beauty without taking that acknowledgment in sinful directions. And those sinful directions include the obvious ones, like undressing a women in one's mind or sexually fantasizing about her.

But the sinful direction might be more subtle. A man might recognize a woman's beauty and begin to imagine what it would be like to be married to her, without it initially being sexual at all. He might follow his aroused curiosity and be enticed into imagining another life, one in which he's married to this woman rather than his wife. Indulging that kind of fantasy is a sin. Running through a scenario in which you're married to your neighbor's wife is a sin. In fact, it made the Ten Commandments. But rightly resisting covetousness and lust requires rightly recognizing covetousness and lust. And so we make the distinction between a normal recognition of beauty and a leaning in, a craving, a coveting, a lusting in one's heart. There's a difference between saying, "She's attractive," and, "I will now fantasize about her." The latter requires more intentionality. It requires the mind to follow the passions of the flesh. It requires the rider to relinquish control and allows the elephant to lead wherever it wants. When we experience the automatic and immediate recognition of female beauty, then the questions are: Do we dive into that bodily reaction, or do we redirect it? Do we twist the recognition of beauty, or do we acknowledge it and move on?

A man has to learn to make these sorts of distinctions and live in light of them. And this is much more difficult if his mind and heart have been shaped by indulging in pornography. As we've explored in previous chapters, long-term porn use creates brain ruts; it shapes how we see the world. We become habituated to viewing all women in a particularly sexualized way. As a result, a man who has been shaped by pornography never simply sees women as attractive; he sees women as lust objects without even trying. He's conditioned himself so that recognition of beauty slides straight into lust. His mind and imagination simply go there. And so, making and living by these distinctions is hard for him.

What's more, if a man carries this way of seeing into marriage, then it becomes difficult for his wife to embrace and live by these biblical distinctions as well. The damage to the marriage means that she views all attractive women as threats, and her instinct will be to remove and neutralize all threats. But a wife's security in her marriage will not ultimately come from the total removal of temptation. Rather, it will come when she is able to rest in the sovereign goodness of the Lord and recognize that she cannot control her husband's wandering eye. Only God can restore to him the kind of self-mastery that, under the influence of the Holy Spirit, is able to calmly and stably recognize the beauty around him and move on.

Finally, just as the watchdog and caged animal can have significant and harmful effects on a church community, so also a healthy church culture is a powerful means in reshaping the distorted imaginations of the individuals within it. A man must learn to relate to other women in the church as sisters, mothers, and daughters in Christ, with all of the appropriate boundaries implied by these relationships. Making small talk at a church picnic, ordinary conversation in a small group, double dates with another couple—all of these can be used by God to reorient the way both husband and wife view members of the opposite sex. As always, personal holiness is a community project.

A Word to Mentors

The Power of Community

When it comes to cultivating healthy community with members of the opposite sex, it's important to recognize the complexity of such relationships and to maintain the right kind of boundaries. For example, while the Bible does encourage Christians to view one another in familial terms (as brother, sister, father, and mother), it's important to note that these relationships are not merely familial. A sister in Christ is *not* identical to a biological sister. In the most obvious sense, one cannot righteously marry his biological sister. But he can (and ought) to marry a sister in Christ. In normal circumstances a biological brother and sister have decades of lived experience together that makes any kind of romantic relationship impossible to imagine. This is not the case for brothers and sisters in Christ. Paul's exhortations to the church to treat one another like family means we ought to cultivate and seek to approximate the kind of nonromantic, nonerotic relations that exist naturally among members of a biological family. However, the fact that Paul has to exhort us to do so reminds us that it takes wise and concerted effort and that maintaining appropriate boundaries with members of the opposite sex is essential. We should treat young women "as sisters with all purity" (1 Tim. 5:2). At its best, this is what things like the "Billy Graham Rule" ("Never be alone with a woman who is not your wife.") are designed to protect.

At the same time, it's important to recognize the dangers of such protections. Over time, they can fundamentally distort relationships among men and women, preventing them from relating to one another as the family of God. As a leader in your church, you ought to attempt to cultivate healthy community, in which men and women can treat each other with respect and dignity as image bearers of God and brothers and sisters in Christ. Small groups, social gatherings, mingling after church—all of these are opportunities to foster godly and healthy relationships in your church. These kinds of ordinary interactions are an important weapon in the fight against sexual sin. As noted in chapter 7, C. S. Lewis said ordinary female society was an important element in learning to flee sexual immorality for him. It helps men to stop seeing women as objects for sexual gratification, and instead, to see them as human beings.

12

A Word to Married Men— Nuisance Lust and Marital Intimacy

In the previous chapter I stressed the importance of distinguishing sin and temptation. By doing so, we break the cycles of reactivity and restore health and wholeness to the marital relationship. In this chapter we'll look at an additional distinction we need to make, as well as explore the place of marital intimacy in the fight for holiness.

In breaking the cycle of reactivity, not only must we distinguish sin from temptation; we also must distinguish varying degrees of sin. This is another place where the watchdog and caged animal dynamic flattens the distinction. Under its influence we can begin to make false equivalencies. *A double take = lusting in your heart = committing adultery.* We often make this equation because of Christ's words in the Sermon on the Mount. "You have heard that it was said, Do not commit adultery. But I tell you, everyone who looks at a woman lustfully has already committed adultery with her in his heart" (Matt. 5:27–28). *There it is,* we say. Looking with lustful intent = adultery.

But that's not what Jesus says. Looking with lustful intent = adultery *in the heart.* But there's a difference between adultery and adultery in the heart.

Jesus is trying to awaken us to the gravity of sin so that we don't give ourselves a pass on the heart simply because we're obeying at the level of behavior. The pharisaical righteousness he's attacking was content with external obedience. Looking with lustful intent was fine in their minds so long as you didn't go to bed with her. Lusting in the heart was fine so long as it didn't lead to concrete actions. Jesus is correcting that false view of righteousness. God cares about the heart, and the command against adultery includes actions, thoughts, and desires.

But while looking with lustful intent is included in the commandment, it is an overreading to equate looking lustfully with having intercourse with someone other than your wife. The latter is a much graver sin since it requires much more intentional and prolonged effort and because it involves actual sexual union with another person. This means that while both adultery and lust are sins and condemned by Jesus, we must still distinguish them in terms of our response to their presence.

Consider the similar connection that Christ draws between murder and anger. While both anger and murder are sins before God, we don't throw a man in prison for murder simply because he was angry in his heart. An angry man is in danger of hell, but he's not in danger of jail time unless his anger flows forth in actual harmful actions. Similarly, a man who refuses to cut off his hand in the fight for lust is in danger of hell (Matt. 5:29–30), but he hasn't committed adultery until his lustful looking leads to concrete action with a woman.

> God cares about the heart, and the command against adultery includes actions, thoughts, and desires.

Now the flattening of the distinction between desires of the heart and actions with the body is amplified when it's combined with the hyper-vigilance I mentioned earlier. This combination leads to the further unhelpful equation of lust in the heart with the kind of idle curiosity evident in double takes. To be clear, this is *not* to defend double takes. Like I said in the last chapter, a man should resist that kind of curiosity since it easily leads to looking with lustful intent. The double take quickly becomes a lustful or covetous fantasy. Remember, the battle needs to start at the top of the hill, not the bottom. But it's important to distinguish between varying degrees of sin so that we can respond to them appropriately.

This is one of the fundamental problems with the reactive dynamic. Every threat is a nuclear threat. But growing in maturity and holiness means being able to distinguish between a bully with a knife and the threat of nuclear attack. Otherwise, the bully shows up, and both husband and wife go to DefCon 1. "Attractive waitress! Push the red button!" That kind of reactivity, flowing from flattened distinctions, is a trap. It's a scheme of the devil.

Instead, we have to cultivate proportionate responses to varying degrees of sin. And a husband must learn to do this while also recognizing that his past failures may make smaller sins feel much larger to his wife. A double take feels much more serious to her if he has used porn in the last few months. And a wise husband who is attempting to pursue holiness and care for his wife will both understand and sympathize with her feelings while resisting the temptation to flatten everything down. Flattening may provide relief in the short run, but in the long run it will be more destructive.

Calm Down

Breaking the cycle of reactivity requires two seemingly opposite actions on the part of a husband. On the one hand, when faced with temptation, he needs to calm down. On the other hand, he can't be lazy or put his pursuit of holiness on autopilot. Both are crucial: chill the heck out, *and* don't coast. When it comes to chilling out, I've been helped by Doug Wilson's counsel for what he calls "nuisance lust." I'll adapt a scenario from Wilson to make the point. Imagine that you're sitting at your computer and you click a link to a news article that interests you. When you get to the news site, the banners on the sidebar are filled with racy celebrity photos and provocative advertisements. Now imagine three different responses to this phenomenon, with your wife invisibly observing you for all of them.

> **Response 1:** You ogle and stare and scroll through the provocative images for a half hour.
>
> **Response 2:** You slam the computer shut, throw it across the room, and call down curses on the news organization in question.
>
> **Response 3:** You see the images, react with a "huh," and then scroll down and finish the article.

Now when we ask which response your wife would prefer, number 2 jumps out. To her the intensity of your response reveals the proper, blood-earnest hunger for holiness and purity. Response 1 is just sin, and there's no excuse. Response 3 awakens some anxiety because "Why didn't you *flee*? Why did you stay on the website? Where was your zeal for your holiness and your marriage?"

Now I'm sympathetic to that way of thinking, and if the choice is between Response 1 and Response 2, I'll take the second every time. But in my mind the long-term goal is much more like Response 3 than either of the others. This is because the high reactivity of Response 2 reveals a kind of sensitivity and susceptibility to temptation that is dangerous because it masquerades behind the reactive intensity. But we want something better than reactive intensity. We want measured stability. We want self-mastery. We want deliberate and intentional hostility that is able to wisely *minimize* the seriousness of the temptation, not in order to indulge our sinful appetites but in order that we can, by the Spirit, *walk away*.

Thus, my counsel to couples who are working through this sort of thing is first, to calm down. I want to help them learn to *respond* to temptation and sin rather than to *react* to temptation and sin. Reactions are impulsive; the passions are just triggered and get out of control in a hurry. Responses are measured; we act intentionally with wisdom because we are under control. As Wilson says, it's the difference between reacting "like a horny and conflicted twelve-year old boy" and responding to nuisance lust like a mature adult. Many couples have to learn that their reactive patterns of failure, fear, and hypervigilance are actually exacerbating the problem rather than helping it. Once we de-escalate and consider the situation soberly, we can have the type of wise, honest, guided conversations that will lead to long-term restoration and holiness.

Don't Coast

The flip side of "chill out" is "don't coast." De-escalating the immediate threat of nuisance lust isn't a license to sin. We don't coast to holiness; we pursue it. And the pursuit of holiness is a community project. Hidden sins kill Christians because they're hidden. We want to get our sins and struggles out on the table so that we can all shoot at them. This means embracing healthy accountability with one's wife and with other godly men. There's a delicate balance to including one's wife in this fight. On the one hand, she can be a valuable asset; she cares about her husband's holiness in this area as much as anyone, and her awareness in times of temptation can lead to fruitful intimacy. On the other hand, her involvement can sometimes unhelpfully raise the temperature in the room, especially if she doesn't experience temptation in the way her husband does. One way to resolve that tension is to allow her to suggest godly men to act as accountability and wisdom in the fight. If she knows that her husband is confessing sin and seeking counsel from men that she trusts, she won't have to be his watchdog. Instead, she'll be free to be his wife.

The goal is to find men who will be as hard on us as God is but who also understand the complexity of sexual temptation and sin. That's why I've written this book. I want your church to be filled with men who are equipped to wisely help one another in the fight, who apply the right kind of pressure and relieve the wrong kind of pressure,

who will sniff out excuses and blame shifting while identifying the deeper motivations within and the schemes of the
devil without. A man who has friends and comrades like
these and a wife with whom he can honestly and calmly
discuss this temptation is set up well for the long haul.

The Place of Marital Intimacy

A final area worth discussing is the marriage bed and
its relationship to the fight with lust and sexual sin. This
is a particularly fraught and emotional subject, with dangers in every direction. So let's start with some basics. If
a man has a history of porn use, it's vital that he grasp
the damage he's done to his marriage, and in particular to
his wife's desire for intimacy with him. Part of living with
her in an understanding way is recognizing the devastation
caused by his sin and the likelihood that she'll need space
in order to heal from the wounds caused by lust and pornography. If you find yourself in this position, it's important to freely give your wife the space she needs to recover
from the news of your failure to honor the marriage bed.
Immediately pressuring her for intimacy will likely exacer-
bate the distance between you. Far better for you to demonstrate fidelity over time in order to earn back her trust
and respect so that sexual intimacy takes its rightful place
in a healthy marriage rather than being a Band-Aid over
the gaping wound of a damaged one. This is another place
where a wise mentor (and his wife) can be of great help.

At the same time, Paul is clear that marriage is one of the key defenses against sexual immorality of all kinds (1 Cor. 7:2). A husband ought to give his wife her conjugal rights, and a wife ought to give her husband his conjugal rights. As one flesh, each of their bodies belongs to the other. Thus, they should not deprive each other of sexual intimacy except by agreement for a limited time in order to devote themselves to prayer (giving her space to heal after your failure being one example of that type of agreement). But after a limited period of abstinence, a husband and a wife should come together again so that Satan doesn't tempt them beyond their self-control (v. 5). The reason for this is obvious—marriage is the proper context for sexual intimacy. As Paul says, "It is better to marry than burn with desire" (v. 9). Sexual passion should lead us to marriage, where its flame can burn bright and clear in its proper place. Marriage is the hearth that houses the fire of sexual intimacy.

A Common Pattern

With that in mind, I want to conclude this chapter on marriage by describing a common marital pattern that frequently fuels temptation of various kinds. Often, in the early days of marriage, a couple can't keep their hands off each other. During dating and engagement, faithfully holding back was actually one of the chief challenges. But over time things begin to change. Kids arrive on the scene, bringing all of the joys and exhaustion that come with parenting. Pregnancy and childbirth alter a woman's body in numerous ways. Even the simple fact of aging affects our interest and desire in sex. The problem is that these factors often affect husbands and wives in different ways. The result is that husbands and wives begin to "miss" each other when it comes to their desires and expectations for sexual intimacy. A husband may watch in confusion as his wife's sexual desire seems to dwindle. He may grow frustrated at the infrequency of intimacy. A wife may learn that the slightest hint of sexual availability on her part awakens her husband's interest. And, because of all of the pressing obligations of family life, she may subtly close herself off sexually so as not to awaken his desire. On the other hand, a husband who showed remarkable romantic capacities during dating, engagement, and the early years of marriage may begin to neglect the fuel of love—conversation, emotional pursuit, romance—and really pursue his wife only when he wants to "have sex." As a result, his wife naturally begins to feel used, closing herself off to his advances even more.

Whatever factors contribute, the end result is that the frequency and nature of lovemaking becomes a matter of subtle and often unspoken negotiations, with husband and wife each withholding what the other wants in order to extract what they each want. And this sort of dynamic is a hotbed of smoldering resentment, frustration, and self-righteousness. No wife wants to beg for conversation and romance. No husband wants to beg for lovemaking. Even being required to ask for such things directly feels wrong to us, like we're cheap and needy. Part of the glory of sex lies in the subtleties of the romantic dance, in foreplay in all of its facets, in the tacit and implicit ways we make known our desires and interest—the slightly raised eyebrow, the knowing glance, the sly smile, the passing touch designed to gauge interest, all mixed together with a playfulness that masks the importance of what's at stake. Solomon says that the way of a man with a maid is a wonderful mystery. Lover and beloved. Pursuer and pursued. When we step into these roles, we inhabit our masculinity and our femininity in a special and mysterious way. It's one of the reasons people commit adultery; for a brief moment they feel the thrill of being a man and a woman, lover and beloved, again. This isn't to excuse adulteries (or pornography, which often mimics this dynamic at the level of imagination and fantasy); it's to explain part of their appeal so that we can inoculate ourselves against their pull.

To that end, it's important to underline that marital intimacy and lovemaking are never merely about bodily union and physical release. Deep emotional, relational, and spiritual undercurrents are in play, and part of growing in wisdom and maturity is learning to cultivate the fullness of the mystery of the one-flesh union. At a practical level this means that husbands must pursue their wives intentionally and holistically; they must *know* their wives in all senses of that word. Conversation, romance, delight in her as a woman, not to mention the provision, protection, and strength that mark a godly head—all of these are crucial in cultivating a healthy marriage, with marital intimacy as the consummation of this comprehensive union of persons.

On the other hand, a wife must recognize that her sexual desire and interest in her husband has a deep impact on his felt sense of his own masculinity. By communicating her availability to him and her desire for him, she is loving and honoring him as her head. What's more, she is encouraging him to step up and be a man, to pursue her, to provide for her and the children she bears for him so that the fire of love at the heart of their home burns bright and clear.

Living this out is not easy, especially if you've dishonored the marriage bed by your lust and sin, or if you feel stuck in the negotiation phase of marital intimacy. How much space to give to your wife after failure is a matter of wisdom. So is getting unstuck when bitterness, entitlement, and resentment have settled in on a marriage because of the unspoken expectations that we harbor in our hearts. This again is one place where honest and open conversation, guided by wise and faithful pastors and mentors (and their wives) can be of great benefit. My hope and prayer is that these chapters can provide a good baseline for such conversations.

A Word to Mentors

The Power of Guided Conversations

At some point in trying to shepherd your men, you will likely also need to shepherd the wives who have been deeply hurt by their husbands' sexual sin. One effect of a husband's porn use is to make it easy for his wife to mistrust all men (including pastors and mentors). This is where your own wife (if you're married) can be of immense help. She will likely be able to identify and connect with the pain and anger of a hurting wife and draw her out in the discussion. She may also be able to explain some of the distinctions from this book in a way that will make sense to another woman. It may be helpful to meet together as couples in order to discuss the struggle. This will provide a place for a wife to ask questions and to ensure that the men in her husband's life are really committed to his holiness.

One possibility is to have the wives of men in your group read through this book and write down questions as they go. There will likely be places where the concepts are unclear or the strategies may not make sense. Encourage men to attempt to have conversations about these things with their wives. Remind them that it's normal to get stuck. At that point a double date in which you and your wife work through the questions with them may help bring them to one mind about the best ways to pursue holiness.

13

A Final Exhortation

In this final chapter I thought it would be helpful to review the overall paradigm and give a few closing exhortations. Walking by the Spirit is the banner that flies over all of our efforts at holiness. Walking by the Spirit is the lifestyle and conduct that flow from believing the good news of Jesus Christ. We walk by the Spirit when we rely on the Spirit to wisely kill sin and pursue holiness. Christ Jesus came into the world to save sinners not only from the penalty of sin but also from the power of sin. Walking by the Spirit involves the whole person, body and mind. We seek to renew the mind and reorient the body as we present ourselves and our members to God as those who have been united to the crucified and risen Christ.

A crucial factor in learning to walk by the Spirit is the gospel presence of a wise mentor. Gospel presence includes both compassionate stability that leans into the struggles of broken sinners and a focused hostility that gives their sin no quarter. Safe for sinners, not for sin. With his words and presence, the mentor calls the men to take responsibility for themselves, to grow up into maturity, to refuse to wallow in guilt and shame, to maintain hope when things get hard, to calm them down when fear and anxiety rage. The mentor is a model for where the men are headed, and his gospel presence is a potent weapon in the hand of the Almighty.

When it comes to the fight itself, the first step is to establish artificial boundaries, particularly in relation to technology, that both gauge a man's seriousness and create space for the heart work to begin. Ideally these barriers are temporary crutches until God restores a man's legs so that he can truly walk by the Spirit. Once the tone has been set with this initial step, we settle in for the long haul, praying violent but hopeful prayers that God will do a great work in our lives. As we seek to untangle the mess sin has made, we recognize that there are layers to this fight. There's a bodily dimension, involving endorphins and dopamine and neural pathways and hormonal polydrugs. Porn use creates brain ruts that weaponize the body against holiness, making porn easy and obedience hard. But the body's plasticity means these sinful habits can be undone as we are renewed in our minds and recatechized in our understanding of men and women and sex. Our goal is to strengthen the rider so that he can faithfully steer the powerful elephant.

A chief part of the mentor's role is to explore the patterns of a man's sin. Lust is never isolated; it's intertwined with other sins, struggles, and sorrows so that we're always engaged in a wider war. Not only are more sins involved, but deeper sins and brokenness are involved, including those that reach back to the formative years of childhood. Because sin is parasitic, we are often trying to identify the true good that is being corrupted and then to redirect our desires to that good in the way God designed. As we explore these patterns, we're also aware of the relational dynamics that contribute to temptation. A man's relationship with his parents, his siblings, his wife, his friends, his work, his church—all of these play a role in a man's pursuit of holiness. Often victory over sexual sin comes in part from repentance, healing, and restoration in some other area of his life. Lust was stealing the headlines, but something else was funding the newspaper.

We recognize progress in the fight with lust as we begin to resist sin at an earlier stage of temptation. Sin is subtle, and where we choose to fight is where the battle will be fought. Often this means engaging at the level of the imagination, repenting of idle fantasies, cultivating a healthy enjoyment of the things of earth, and redirecting our imagination toward things that are good, true, and beautiful. In particular, we engage in "good pretending," in which we consider ourselves dead to sin and alive to God in Christ, imagining what we would do if we were full of Jesus, asking for God's help, and then doing it.

There are particular challenges to men at different stages of life. Young men must learn to cultivate self-control and self-mastery. Engaged men are seeking to demonstrate that they are trustworthy by refusing to sin against their future wives with their current fiancés. Married men must learn to navigate the difficult waters of this struggle with their wives, who are often hurt and wounded by past failures. They must learn to break the cycle of reactivity by making proper distinctions, by chilling the heck out, and by not coasting. A healthy marriage is a powerful weapon in the pursuit of holiness.

Finally, let me close with an exhortation. Walking by the Spirit is not easy, but it's worth it. Don't grow weary in doing good. Recognize that this is a lifelong fight, and don't despair when you face setbacks. Learning to fight *your* sin is an experimental science. We're bringing to bear the Word of God, the Spirit of God, and our own sanctified wisdom to try to learn our patterns, break them down, and rebuild them in holy ways. Don't be passive when it comes to this fight. Be active and intentional. Gouge out the eye. Cut off your hand. Take every thought captive and make it obedient to Jesus. Don't allow little sins to fester. Don't allow the devil to gain a foothold. When you stumble, confess it to God to receive forgiveness, confess it to other men to receive healing and counsel, and then, when necessary, confess it to your wife to restore the covenant. Don't get stuck. Instead, plow through failure. Those failures are opportunities to grow, to learn your patterns, to explore your deeper motivations so that God can restore control of you to you.

And remember, we are pursuing holiness. That is to say, we are pursuing *joy*. In God, holiness and happiness are the same thing. The Holy Spirit is the happy Spirit, the blessed Spirit, the joyful Spirit. Walk by him, and you won't gratify the desires of the flesh.

Appendix:
Further Resources

The following list of articles and books have helped me develop my eclectic approach to helping men win the battle against sexual sin. I include the author, title, and a brief description. I also link each resource to the relevant chapter(s) in this book.

Articles

Matthew Lee Anderson, "How Pornography Makes Us Less Human and Less Humane," *Christian Living*, August 26, 2019, https://www.thegospelcoalition.org/article/pornography-human-humane/.

A substantial look at the dehumanizing effects of pornography. Topics include the danger of ravenous curiosity, the objectification of people, and the death of wonder produced by porn.

Joe Carter, "9 Things You Should Know about Pornography and the Brain," *Christian Living*, May 8, 2013, https://www.thegospelcoalition.org/article/9-things-you-should-know-about-pornography-and-the-brain/.

A brief article explaining the effects of pornography on the brain. Contains a number of links to longer articles and videos with more detail (chapter 4).

Tim Challies, "I Looked for Love In Your Eyes," *Challies*, December 18, 2010, https://www.challies.com/quotes/i-looked-for-love-in-your-eyes/.
A deeply moving poem by an anonymous woman, grieving the effect of her husband's porn use on their marriage and children (chapter 4).

Jason DeRouchie, "If Your Right Hand Causes You to Sin: Ten Reflections on Masturbation," *Desiring God*, December 3, 2016, https://www.desiringgod.org/articles/if-your-right-hand-causes-you-to-sin.
A Bible-saturated article addressing the challenge of masturbation.

Pascal Emanuel-Gobry, "A Science-Based Case for Ending the Porn Epidemic," *American Greatness*, December 15, 2019, https://amgreatness.com/2019/12/15/a-science-based-case-for-ending-the-porn-epidemic.
A deep dive into the latest research on the porn epidemic and its social consequences (chapter 4).

Andrew David Naselli, "Seven Reasons You Should Not Indulge in Pornography." *w* 41.3 (2016): 473–83, http://andy-naselli.com/wp-content/uploads/2016_pornography.pdf.

An article that exposes the pervasive connection between pornography and sex trafficking and sex slavery (chapter 4).

Alastair Roberts, "Man and Woman in Creation (Genesis 1 and 2)," *Preaching & Theology*, December 10, 2019, https://www.9marks.org/article/man-and-woman-in-creation-genesis-1-and-2/.

An article that explores what it means to be made in God's image as men and women (chapter 3).

William M. Struthers, "The Effects of Porn on the Male Brain," *CRI*, March 18, 2020, https://www.equip.org/article/the-effects-of-porn-on-the-male-brain-3/.

An article-length synopsis of Struther's book that focuses on the Big 5 chemicals involved in pornography (chapter 4).

Doug Wilson, "Nuisance Lust," *Blog & Mablog*, September 6, 2010, https://dougwils.com/books/dealing-with-nuisance-lust.html

A helpful article for men who have been freed from pornography and are seeking to walk faithfully in a sexualized world and need help communicating with their wives (chapter 12).

Books

David Powlison, *Making All Things New: Restoring Joy to the Sexually Broken.* Wheaton, IL: Crossway, 2017.

A short but wise book on renewing our sexuality. Powlison focuses both on fighting sexual sin and healing from sexual trauma. His work has influenced my own ministry in significant ways (chapters 5–9).

Jay Stringer, *Unwanted: How Sexual Brokenness Reveals Our Way to Healing.* Colorado Springs, CO: NavPress, 2018.

A fantastic book that explores the ways our formative childhood experiences and present life struggles influence the patterns of unwanted sexual behavior (chapter 8).

William Struthers, *Wired for Intimacy: How Pornography Hijacks the Male Brain.* Downers Grove, IL: IVP Books, 2009.

A book-length treatment from a Christian neuroscientist that addresses both the mental and the bodily dimension of pornography (chapter 4).

Douglas Wilson, *Fidelity: How to Be a One-Woman Man.* Moscow, ID: Canon Press, 1999.

A clear, straightforward book about the threats to fidelity and the marriage bed in our day, written to men and their sons (chapters, 4, 11, and 12).